PCC

ACCOUNTABILITY

The Charities Act 2011 and the PCC

4th edition

Guidance on accounts, reports and scrutiny including the
Church Accounting Regulations 2006 prescribed by the Business
Committee of the General Synod

Church House
Great Smith Street
London
SW1P 3AZ

ISBN 978–0–7151–1065-2

First published 2006 by
Church House Publishing.

Fourth edition published in 2013
for the House of Bishops of the
General Synod of the Church
of England

Typeset by ForDesign
Printed and bound by
CPI Group (UK) Ltd,
Croydon, CR0 4YY

Contents

Part 1

Accruals Accounting

chapter 1

Introduction and Legal Overview

1.1 Background

This publication has been designed to provide all users with a comprehensive and up-to-date reference guide to assist in the preparation of the requisite PCC annual report and accounts. The content has been updated in the light of current legislation and replaces the two previous publications:

The Charities Act 1993 and the PCC: Preparing Receipts and Payment Accounts (SORP 2005) and
The Charities Act 1993 and the PCC 3rd edition: A guide to the SORP 2005 revisions

The book is divided into two distinct sections and the reader can select whichever is relevant, depending on whether they are producing accounts on a receipts and payments basis or are adopting accrual accounting. The following flow chart is the starting point and should be used to determine which method should be adopted. The appendices provide a guide to moving from one method of accounting to another, sample accounts and extracts from relevant legislation.

This revision of the guide has been produced by sub-groups of the Diocesan Accounts Group. The sub-groups comprise representation from diocesan and national church staff and external professional advisers. The members of the sub-groups are acknowledged at the back of this guide.

The content of this book is accessible online on the Church of England's Parish Resources website at: www.parishresources.org.uk

Further guidance can be found on the Charity Commission website at: www.charity-commission.gov.uk

Another useful source of guidance is the Association of Church Accountants and Treasurers (ACAT). This is a national charity which provides resources to support the work of treasurers in churches of all Christian denominations. ACAT provides a programme of training events including foundation courses for new treasurers and more detailed workshops on specific topics which are relevant to PCC governance and financial administration. Further information is available on ACAT's website: www.acat.uk.com

1.2 Regime of public accountability

There are two different bases for the preparation of annual financial statements, depending on the size of the PCC in terms of gross annual income. There are also two different forms of external scrutiny of the financial statements.

The requirements and options are summarised on the following flow chart.

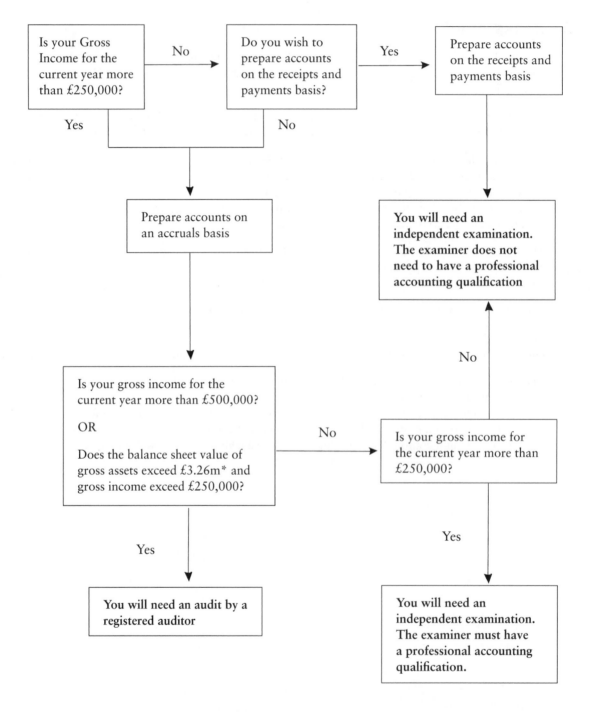

*Gross assets exclude benefice properties (parsonages), consecrated land and buildings and moveable church furnishings. These items are not included in PCC accounts.

Making the choice

This section describes whether accounts on the Receipts & Payments or accruals accounting basis must or may be prepared.

1.3   How large is your PCC?

In order to discover which aspects of the Regulations apply to the PCC, its statutory 'gross income' must first be calculated according to the Charity Commission's rules. The PCC can then identify where it stands in the accounting framework for charity accounts.

The Charity Commission's rules for calculating gross income allow you to do this by reference to cash receipts as long as the figure of £250,000 is not exceeded. If it is exceeded you will have to prepare accounts on the accruals basis, even if this would result in showing a gross income figure of less than £250,000 in the Statement of Financial Activities (SOFA).

1.4   What is the 'gross income' of the PCC for the purposes of Receipts and Payments accounts?

The gross income is the total recorded income of the PCC in all unrestricted and restricted funds but not amounts received as capital (endowment) funds, nor amounts in respect of the disposal or revaluation of fixed assets held for investment or the PCC's own use. Gross income should be recorded before the deduction of any costs or expenses and includes the following (the list of items in Chapter 4 will help to identify income items).

- Voluntary income

- Gross proceeds of activities for generating funds

- Investment income receipts

- Receipts from charitable activities and

- Any expendable endowment spent as income or transferred to income funds and any unapplied total return allocated or transferred to income funds during the year (this latter is unlikely to arise in practice for small charities).

The following items should be **excluded**:

- a loan received by the PCC;

- the repayment to the PCC of a loan made by them;

- the proceeds of the sale of investments or 'functional fixed assets' (such as a hall, which is held for the purpose of furthering the mission of the church) or any gain or profit on their sale;

- donations received by the PCC with the specific requirement that they be held as endowments (i.e. the income can be used by the PCC and would be shown as in the guidance above, but the primary endowment would not be included).

The table below summarises the gross income of the PCC.

Include	Exclude
Voluntary income	
• All donations from individuals • Grants from organisations	• Grants conditional upon the achievement of certain criteria which have not yet been met • Grants promised but not yet received • Donations received as capital (endowment) funds where only the income can be used by the PCC • Loans received by the PCC • Repayment to the PCC of a loan made by them
Proceeds of activities for generating funds	
• Gross income before the deduction of any costs or expenses incurred	• Associated expenses that are very small (not material) and where it is impractical to identify them separately
Investment income	
• Interest on deposit accounts • Dividends paid both in cash and shares • Investment income derived from endowment funds	• Revaluation gains • Proceeds of the sale of investments or 'functional fixed assets' e.g. a hall or curate's house held for the purpose of furthering the mission of the church • Profits on the sale of investments or functional fixed assets
Income from charitable activities	
• Gross income before the deduction of any costs or expenses e.g. heating	• Amounts received on behalf of other parties e.g. verger, organist, choir that are to be paid straight out again • Assigned fees collected on behalf of the clergy and diocese

Where a PCC holds endowment funds then any expendable endowment spent or transferred to income funds and any unapplied total return allocated or transferred to income funds during the year should also be included in the gross income calculation.

Further detail of the various items of income is given in Chapter 4.

Points to note

● If the calculation of statutory gross income is being made from financial statements prepared on the accruals basis, then the starting point for this is the SOFA's 'incoming resources' sub-totals in the unrestricted and restricted income funds columns only. From this, any unrealised gain within 'other income' from the disposal of any functional fixed assets used for the work of the PCC should be excluded.

● In calculating the gross income, there should be no netting off of expenditure and income (no cancelling income against expenditure). Suppose the parish runs a fete and raises £1,000 after charging £500 for expenses. They should show £1,500 of income and £500 of expenditure. If the netting off is small and it is impracticable to identify the precise amount, then this requirement to 'gross up' can be ignored.

- If in doubt, include an item rather than leave it out. The rules are to help people to understand the financial statements more easily and to help PCCs have the information they need for managing their affairs properly. These aims should be kept in mind when deciding which small items should be included or excluded, either gross or net.

- Insurance claims are cost reimbursements which may be netted off against expenditure made, in effect, on behalf of the insurers, to the extent that they do not include a profit or gain element which must be recognised as such in the SOFA (e.g. 'new for old' or 'rainy day' insurance) and do not count as an 'income receipt' for accounting purposes (e.g. when shown in a Receipts and Payments Account). Where the insurer pays a supplier's bill direct (as is often the case with vehicle damage claims) that amount should not be shown as revenue expenditure nor as income (fixed asset replacement entails different accounting rules).

- Money may be received to build a new building or to improve an existing building. If the funds raised create an endowment (due to the nature of the gift) or the asset to be improved is an endowment asset the funds raised are endowment and should be excluded from the calculation of gross income.

- If there is a major appeal for activities or repair or a major non-endowed legacy is received in a year it will be quite possible for the gross income in that year to increase from, say, £100,000 to over £250,000. If this happens, no attempt must be made to manipulate the figures by artificially accelerating or delaying activities. As the PCC will be handling larger sums of money it is only right that it should have to account for them in a more rigorous way.

- The law requires all gross income to be included (e.g. also any occasional non-endowed legacies and grants), even if its inclusion makes the financial size of the parish much bigger than was previously the case and than the PCC expects. The calculations are made to arrive at a figure of genuine gross income.

Legal overview

This section provides an overview of the requirements of the Charities Act 2011 and associated regulations (see Appendix iii) and relates them to both large and small Parochial Church Councils (PCCs).

1.5 The duties of the PCC

The members of the PCC are the charity trustees and are the 'persons having the general control and management of the administration of the charity' (Charities Act 2011, s177).

The trustees are entrusted with the PCC's funds. They must:

- always act responsibly;

- ensure that all decisions are taken for the benefit of the PCC;

- always act in accordance with the governing documents, principally the Parochial Church Councils (Powers) Measure 1956;

- not seek personal benefit (commitment to the cause must be the main reason for serving as a trustee).

The PCC is responsible for all parish finance, its management and control, including the appointment of a treasurer. While it may delegate some of its duties, for example, to District Church Councils (DCCs), this does not remove its legal responsibilities. These include:

- Keeping 'proper accounting records', which include the annual financial statements, and which must be preserved for at least six years from the end of the financial year to which they relate. The records must be sufficient to:

  - show and explain all the PCC's transactions;

  - disclose the PCC's financial position at any time with reasonable accuracy;

- enable the required accounts to be prepared;

- show on a day-to-day basis all receipts and payments and what they were for;

- record all assets and liabilities.

● Ensuring that the finances of the PCC are under its control and decision making is only delegated if the PCC can ensure that its wishes will be followed.

● Arranging for a suitable independent examination or audit of the financial statements.

● Preparing the annual report and accounts (financial statements), which must be presented to the Annual Parochial Church Meeting in accordance with the requirements of the Church Representation Rules.

1.6 Accounting framework

The accounting, auditing and reporting regime for almost all charities, including Church of England PCCs, is contained in the following documentation:

● *Charities Act 2011*
This represents a consolidation of the Charities Acts 1993 and 2006 and other acts but did not introduce any new legislation.

Section 145 (5) of the 2011 Act empowers the Charity Commission to issue guidance on the selection of independent examiners and statutory directions to them.

● *Charities (Accounts and Reports) Regulations 2008*
This gives power to the Charity Commission to issue dispensation from the Act's audit/independent examination requirements in specified circumstances.

● *Statement of Recommended Practice on Accounting and Reporting by Charities (SORP 2005)*
Although it is technically 'recommended' SORP 2005 is effectively mandatory for all non-exempt charities preparing accruals accounts to show a 'true and fair view', and provides an appropriate framework for all such charities, large and small.

● *Financial Reporting Standard for Smaller Entities (FRSSE)*
The composite financial reporting standard that PCCs are eligible to adopt as part of their accounting policies. This standard applies only to the PCC's own accounts and not to any group consolidated accounts (see Chapter 7).

In addition, financial statements for PCCs must be prepared in accordance with the following:

● *The Parochial Church Councils (Powers) Measure*

● *The Church Representation Rules (CRRs)*

● *The Church Accounting Regulations 2006*, which form the link between the CRRs and the requirements of the Charities Act.

The law makes it clear that charities are accountable to the public for the resources they control. Charities receive funds for public benefit and must demonstrate to the public that they have observed the trust placed in them in the handling and use of those funds.

Under the Charities Act 2011, all PCCs below the special registration threshold (currently £100,000 per annum) are excepted charities and do not have to file annual returns or annual reports and accounts with the Charity Commission. Details of the registration process for PCCs over this threshold are available on the Parishes Resources website (www.parishresources.org).

All PCCs must prepare their annual report and financial statements in accordance with the Charities Act 2011 and the regulations and, as with any other charity, must make them available to the public.

1.7 Accounting for the legal entity

The general principle is that statutory accounts must be produced for the legal entity.

That means that PCCs (as the legal entity) must prepare appropriate annual reports and accounts that are in accordance with the Charities Act and the Charities (Accounts & Reports) Regulations, as applicable, and this responsibility cannot be delegated to others.

This is quite straightforward in most cases but questions arise when considering teams, united benefices and pluralities.

1.8 United benefices and pluralities

In the case of united benefices and pluralities, each PCC must produce accounts in the statutory format.

The thresholds are tested for each PCC, which must each appoint an independent examiner or, if appropriate, an auditor. Providing the independence test holds good, the same person may agree to serve more than one PCC.

1.9 Teams

Teams vary a great deal and the guidance on how to meet the requirements of the Charities Act varies with the circumstances. For example:

● Teams which comprise a number of separate PCCs must produce separate accounts that meet the statutory requirements at the level of each PCC. Of course a summary financial statement can be produced at the level of the team, but there is no requirement to do so and there are no constraints on the format.

● Other teams may have been formed on the basis of a single parish comprising one PCC with more than one place of worship but without DCCs. As before, accounts that meet the statutory requirements must be produced for the PCC. Of course there is nothing to stop the production of non-statutory financial statements that in each case relate to one of the different congregations with its place of worship, but there is no requirement to do so and there are no constraints on the format. It may be appropriate for such information to take the form of notes to the PCC accounts (so that they are part of that body of statutory information).

1.10 District Church Councils (DCCs)

A situation may arise where pastoral re-organisation has combined separate parishes into a new single parish and thus a single PCC with DCCs as its 'branches' to retain the sense of local community.

In this case statutory accounts must be produced at the level of the PCC, though these can of course be based on the aggregation of 'branch' accounts that may be produced by the DCCs for their own congregations.

While certain internal management responsibilities can be passed down from the PCC to its DCCs, this does not amount to delegated legal and financial responsibility which must by law stay with the PCC as the only body with legal standing. DCCs cannot have assets of their own, they do not have body corporate status like the PCC nor are they legally distinct from it and so they should not be taking financial decisions and signing contracts, for which they lack the requisite legal standing. Of course the PCC can decide to leave DCCs free to operate within an agreed budget, but the PCC is the only legal entity that is able to enter into a contract or institute legal proceedings.

Where DCCs have been preparing their own accounts there is no reason why this should not continue, but these are then only 'branch' accounts, to be brought together at the PCC level to form the latter's statutory accounts, and therefore careful coordination between the DCCs and the PCC over the final examination/audit of the PCC's statutory accounts will be needed.

1.11 Aggregation of PCC and DCC accounts

If the DCCs have been used to preparing and publishing their own, separate accounts, the need to aggregate the accounts at PCC level may be a cause for concern to them. Consideration of the following may mitigate the circumstances for them:

- If the DCCs are very small and the PCC of which they form a part is below the accruals accounts threshold, the statutory requirements should be relatively easily met by taking the receipts and payments accounts for the individual DCCs and preparing a combined statement of receipts and payments to go with the PCC's statement of all assets and liabilities. An annual report will be required at PCC level which could have general details for the PCC and short reports on activities from each DCC.

- If the aggregated gross income exceeds £250,000 per annum then the statutory requirement is for a single statement of accounts on the accruals basis covering all the DCCs and other transactions at PCC level. It should be noted that if the income threshold of £500,000pa is exceeded there is an audit requirement.

- The independent examiner's task may appear onerous but the person responsible for the examination does not have to carry it all out themselves. The PCC will need to appoint an independent examiner (who will need to meet the requirements of the task) but the examiner might choose to delegate aspects of the work to others, particularly if a number of congregations have to be covered. In this way each DCC may have its part of the aggregated accounts examined by a different person, but the DCC examiners would all be working to the PCC's statutory examiner, who will take sole legal responsibility for any work they have been delegated to carry out. It is the PCC examiner who is responsible for agreeing the programme of work of the local examiners, reviewing the results of their work and then reporting in statutory terms on the statutory accounts of the PCC.

It cannot be avoided that aggregation at PCC level may increase the gross income of the PCC to a level which means that it crosses a threshold and enters a more rigorous regime.

It should be noted that a PCC with DCCs does not require a common bank account. The PCC may arrange for each DCC to have its own bank account but this will need to be subject to the overall control of the PCC and subject to an assessment of any risks and benefits of operating multiple bank accounts.

Joint arrangements

Some groups of PCCs operate a group or PCC account, to which PCCs contribute. It is used to fund joint activities, such as the incumbent's working expenses or a magazine. This fund may be accounted for in one of two ways:

- One PCC in the group may control the fund as a restricted fund and receive grants from the other PCCs in the group. This PCC then accounts for the fund and the other PCCs show their contribution as a grant. If the fund is a significant sum of money, the PCC may not wish to adopt this method as it may move them into a more complex accounting regime.

- The joint account may be handled as an informal 'joint venture' (called a 'joint arrangement' in the SORP), where each PCC accounts for its share of the total fund. A PCC treasurer may operate an account, which serves the joint activity. The expenditure on the account should be allocated appropriately to each PCC. The PCC treasurer running the account should not treat payments received from the other PCCs as income. Any assets or liabilities generated within the account also need to be allocated to each contributing PCC at the year-end.

1.12 Local ecumenical partnerships (LEPs)

Where a parish is part of a Local Ecumenical Partnership (LEP), the PCC continues to exercise certain functions in relation to the parish separately from the charity comprising the LEP. This includes the preparation of the financial statements of the PCC – which have to continue to be provided in all cases. Some denominations have a year-end date other than 31 December and the constitution will establish the relevant accounting date for the particular LEP. The constitutions may establish different legal rights and obligations for the participating denominations and the accounting consequences will need to be determined on a case-by-case basis.

1.13 Registration with the Charity Commission or excepted status

The Charities Act 2011 specifies that PCCs and other excepted charities with gross income in excess of a special registration threshold (currently £100,000 per annum) must register with the Charity Commission.

Dispensation from registration can be sought from the Charity Commission where the income threshold of £100,000 per annum has been exceeded only because of an exceptional and non-recurring item.

Details of the registration process are available on the Parish Resources website (www.parishresources.org).

Registered charities must:

● disclose their registration status on all relevant documents, e.g. letterheads, website, cheques, invoices and receipts (e.g. 'a registered charity' or 'Charity No. xxxxxxx');

● submit an Annual Return to the Charity Commission;

● submit a copy of the Annual Report and Accounts to the Charity Commission (unless PCC income has fallen below £25,000 for the year);

Excepted status remains for all PCCs which are not registered with the Charity Commission.

Excepted charities do not have a charity registration number and do not have to file an annual report and accounts with the Commission unless specifically requested.

All PCCs, registered and excepted, must, however (under the Church Representation Rules), send a copy of the Annual Report and Accounts to the Secretary of the Diocesan Board of Finance. They must also be provided to the public upon written request. PCCs are charitable bodies and may, inter alia, claim tax refunds on Gift Aid contributions, receive investment income without deduction of income tax and in general enjoy all the other tax reliefs available to registered charities.

New rules established by HMRC require all charities registering for Gift Aid tax claims to meet the 'fit and proper test' and other requirements.

1.14 Basic overview of PCC accounts

In preparing their accounts PCCs must:

● account for their incoming resources and the investment or expenditure of their resources in at least three main categories: unrestricted funds, restricted funds and endowment funds;

● aggregate the accounts of any other parts of the organisation which the PCC controls;

● account for their stewardship of those resources:

  ● either in cash-based accounts, consisting of receipts and payments account(s) with a Statement of Assets and Liabilities, distinguishing any endowed or other funds restricted under trust law;

  ● or in accruals accounts, which show a true and fair view, consisting of a Statement of Financial Activities, a balance sheet and notes to give certain additional information;

● identify and, if accruals accounts are prepared, put a proper value on their assets, to help the public to understand the PCC's financial position;

● report on their finances and activities in such a way that the general public can understand what has been going on;

● have the accounts scrutinised by an independent examiner if they are not required to be audited by a registered auditor, under the Charities Act and the Church Accounting Regulations.

1.15 Good presentation points

Financial statements should be transparent so that nothing consequential is hidden or obscured, but as uncomplicated as possible so that they may be easily understood.

● **Avoid too much detail**
   Detailed analyses of all the individual accounts, even in the smallest parishes, can be confusing. Only make reference to what is material and round all figures to the nearest pound.

● **Summarise where possible**
   Summarising different funds in columnar format gives the reader a better overall picture. It also allows a reduction in the number of comparative figures.

● **If preparing summarised financial statements**
   A non-statutory summary, derived from the full financial statements, may be produced to help parishioners understand the finances. There are rules about the preparation of summaries in the Charities SORP, which recommends that information about both the Statement of Financial Activities and the Balance Sheet should be included. The full annual report and financial statements should always be available, however.

● **Put any necessary detail in the notes wherever possible**
   The reader is less likely to be confused by the details when looking at the overall picture.

chapter 2

What are Accrual Accounts?

2.1 Accounts structure

The financial statements are a report in financial terms on the activities and resources of the charity, and must comprise:

- A Statement of Financial Activities (SOFA) for the year that shows all incoming resources made available to the PCC and all resources expended by it, and reconciles all movements in its funds (see Chapter 4). The Statement should consist of a single set of accounting statements and be presented in columnar form where the PCC has restricted income or endowment funds.

- A Balance Sheet that shows the assets, liabilities and funds of the charity. SORP 2005 also comments that the Balance Sheet may be presented in columnar format. This is not mandatory but using it ensures a more detailed and therefore informative presentation of the required analysis of assets and liabilities by category of fund (see Chapter 5).The Balance Sheet (or the notes to the financial statements) should also explain in general terms how the funds may or, because of restrictions imposed by donors, must be utilised.

- Notes to the financial statements, explaining the accounting policies adopted and explaining or expanding upon the information contained in the accounting statements referred to above, or which provide further useful information. This will include notes analysing the figures in the primary financial statements and explaining the relationships between them.

- A Cashflow Statement. The largest PCCs which are not eligible for the adoption of the Financial Reporting Standard for Smaller Entities (FRSSE) as their accounting policy, may also have to provide a cash flow statement under the accounting standards. Such parishes will already require a full audit and your auditor will advise accordingly.

The financial statements should include all the money and other assets entrusted to the PCC for whatever purpose, and show how they have been expended during the year and how the unexpended balance of each fund was held at the year-end.

The corresponding figures for the previous year (but only for the PCC as a whole) should be provided in the financial statements in accordance with generally accepted accounting practice, i.e. adjusted where necessary to show them on the same basis as the current year's figures.

2.2 The principle of materiality

Information is material and therefore has relevance if its omission or misstatement could influence the economic decisions of users made on the basis of the financial statements. Transactions or amounts which are clearly insignificant need not be separately shown or explained in the financial statements. As a general rule, a transaction or amount may be treated as insignificant ('immaterial') if it is without doubt too trivial to influence the reader of the financial statements. Too much detail about small items may confuse the overall picture but, if there is doubt about whether or not something is 'material', the information should be included.

2.3 Accounting policies

In order to understand the figures in the financial statements, the reader needs to know the basis on which they have been prepared. The 'accounting policies' note to the financial statements should therefore disclose that the financial statements are prepared under the current Church Accounting Regulations and in accordance with the current Charities SORP and applicable accounting standards (for 2015 onwards, this is expected to become just the current FRSSE for all but the very largest PCCs, which will have to follow FRS102). In addition, the specific accounting policies and assumptions adopted for dealing with any material items should be briefly but clearly explained in the notes to the financial statements. They will include an explanation of the estimation techniques that have been used where judgement is required to record the value of incoming or outgoing resources and of assets and liabilities.

The accounting policies adopted must be those that are considered the most appropriate to the PCC, and so must normally also be consistent with the 'going concern' concept, namely that the PCC is considered to be a going concern for the foreseeable future (normally at least one year from the date of signing the annual report and accounts), and must provide relevant, reliable, comparable and understandable information.

Observance of these fundamental concepts is presumed unless stated otherwise. In addition, the appropriateness of the individual accounting policies and estimation techniques adopted is to be judged by how well they enable the PCC's accruals accounts to achieve the objectives of 'true and fair' financial reporting, as clarified originally in FRS 18 (Accounting Policies) and included in the FRSSE.

Apart from this, the accounting policies note should explain the specific accounting treatment, in each case, of any material items in the financial statements. These will help the reader to understand how matters noted in the following paragraphs have been handled in the financial statements and so they do need to be included if the accounts are to present a true and fair view. A model set of accounting policies is set out below. PCCs should add to and amend these as appropriate for their particular circumstances.

The financial statements should be approved at a meeting of the PCC and the balance sheet signed on the PCC's behalf and the date of approval shown. Only one signature is needed; this is usually that of the chairman of the meeting. However, in the case of the Church of England, where the chairman of the meeting will normally be the minister, it is good practice for the financial statements also to be signed by one other member, normally the treasurer or churchwarden, to underline the joint responsibility of both the minister and members of the PCC.

Model set of accounting policies

PCCs should adapt these as necessary. The accounting policies should be disclosed in the financial statements to assist the reader, particularly in respect of material items.

Basis of preparation

The financial statements have been prepared under the Charities Act 2011 and in accordance with the Church Accounting Regulations 2006 governing the individual accounts of PCCs, together with applicable accounting standards and the Statement of Recommended Practice, Accounting and Reporting by Charities (SORP 2005).

The financial statements have been prepared under the historical cost convention except for the valuation of investment assets, which are shown at market value.

INCOMING RESOURCES

Recognition of incoming resources	These are included in the Statement of Financial Activities (SOFA) when: 1. the PCC becomes legally entitled to the benefit of use of the resources; 2. their ultimate receipt is virtually certain; and 3. the monetary value can be measured with sufficient reliability.
Fund-raising costs	Funds raised from events and trading activities (e.g. a fete, a garden party or sales of books and magazines) are reported gross in the SOFA – i.e., before any related costs that may have been deducted from the gross proceeds.

Grants and donations	Grants and donations are included in the SOFA when any pre-conditions preventing their use by the PCC have been met. For collections and planned giving this is when the funds are received.
Gift Aid Tax claims, etc., on cash donations	Gift Aid and other tax claims are included in the SOFA at the same time as the cash donations to which they relate.
Gifts in kind	Gifts in kind are accounted for at a reasonable estimate of their value at the time of gift to the PCC, if feasible, or else at the amount actually realised from their disposal.
	Gifts in kind for sale to fund the PCC are included in the accounts at their estimated market value at the date of gift, if feasible – or else recognised when sold by the charity.
	Gifts in kind for the PCC's own use are included in the SOFA as incoming resources when receivable, and expensed as and when consumed in use. Gifts of fixed assets, if material, are included in the balance sheet and expensed over the asset's useful economic life.
Donated services and facilities	These are included in incoming resources (and at the same time in resources expended) at the estimated value to the PCC of the service or facility received.
Volunteer help	The value of any voluntary help received is not included in the accounts but is described in the trustees' annual report.
Rental income	Rental income from the letting of the church is recognised when the rental is due.
Investment income	This is included in the accounts when receivable.
Investment gains and losses	This includes any gain or loss on the sale of investments and any gain or loss resulting from revaluing investments to market value at the end of the year.

EXPENDITURE AND LIABILITIES

Liability recognition	Liabilities are recognised as soon as the legal or constructive obligation arises.
Governance costs	Include costs of the preparation and examination of statutory accounts, the costs of trustee meetings and cost of any legal advice to trustees on governance or constitutional matters.
Grants payable without performance conditions	These are recognised in the accounts when a commitment has been made externally and there are no pre-conditions still to be met for entitlement to the grant which remain within the control of the PCC.
Support Costs (If allocated across more than one heading)	Support costs include central functions and have been allocated to activity cost categories on a basis consistent with the use of resources see 2.13.

ASSETS

Consecrated and benefice property	Consecrated and benefice property of any kind is excluded from the financial statements by Section 10(2) (a) and (c) of the Charities Act 2011.

Movable church furnishings	These are capitalised at cost and depreciated over their useful economic life other than where insufficient cost information is available. In this case the item is not capitalised, but all items are included in the Church's inventory in any case.
Tangible fixed assets for use by charity	These are capitalised if they can be used for more than one year, and cost at least £1,000. They are valued at cost or else, for gifts-in-kind, at a reasonable estimate of their open market value on receipt. Depreciation is calculated to write off fixed assets over their estimated useful lives as follows: • Land — Nil • Buildings* — Nil • Fixtures & Fittings — 20 years • Computers — 3 years • Motor vehicles — x years *No depreciation is provided on buildings as the currently estimated residual value of the properties (discounted for monetary inflation since their capitalisation) is not less than their carrying value and the remaining useful life of these assets currently exceeds 50 years, so that any depreciation charges would be immaterial. If the carrying value of the buildings looks greater than their current value on this basis, an impairment review would be carried out and any resultant loss included in expenditure for the year.
Investments	Investments quoted on a recognised stock exchange or whose value derives from them (CIFs, etc.) are valued at market value at the year end. Other investment assets are included at trustees' best estimate of market value.
Trading Stocks	These are valued at the lower of cost or market value.
Short-term deposits	Include cash held on deposit either with the CBF Church of England Funds or at the bank.
FUNDS	
Unrestricted Funds	These represent the remaining income funds of the PCC that are available for spending on the general purposes of the PCC, including amounts designated by the PCC for fixed assets for its own use or for spending on a future project and which are therefore not included in its 'free reserves' as disclosed in the trustees' report.
Restricted Funds	These are income funds that must be spent on restricted purposes and details of the funds held and restrictions provided are shown in the notes to the accounts.
Endowment Funds	These are restricted funds that must be retained as trust capital either permanently or subject to a discretionary power to spend capital as income, and where the use of any income or other benefit derived from the capital may be restricted or unrestricted. Full details of all their restrictions are shown in the notes to the accounts.

Notes to the financial statements: other disclosures

In addition to the disclosure of accounting policies described in this chapter and Chapter 4 further disclosures not relating to the figures are required to support the information in the SOFA and balance sheet. These are detailed below.

2.4 Charitable commitments

An unfulfilled commitment to make a grant or other voluntary contribution to a third party will not normally be a legally binding obligation, but where a valid expectation was created in the mind of the other party as at 31 December, it should be recognised in full as a liability in the financial statements for the year.

Where a PCC has authorised expenditure out of its unrestricted funds without making any external commitment, the PCC may wish to designate unrestricted funds to represent this future expenditure commitment. Any such amounts should be shown separately as designated funds, and clearly explained in the notes to the financial statements. The notes should also explain why the PCC has set up such a fund.

Particulars of all material commitments should be disclosed in the notes if they have not been charged in the financial statements. The note should show the amounts involved, when the commitments are likely to be met and the movements on commitments previously reported.

Where later events make the recognition of liability no longer appropriate, the provision should be cancelled by credit against the relevant expenditure heading in the SOFA. The credit should mirror the treatment originally used to recognise the liability and should be disclosed separately, with a clear explanation in the notes to the financial statements, if material.

Disclosure or provision as appropriate may need to be made for any commitment the PCC may have in relation to the repair and maintenance of non-capitalised fixed assets such as benefice or consecrated property. If these amount to constructive obligations, they will be accounted for as creditors and charged to the SOFA. However, if there is no contractual commitment at the balance sheet date, any funds set aside for repair and maintenance should be regarded as designated funds and not charged to the SOFA. The Annual Report should in any case say when the last quinquennial inspection was held and give details of the immediate works needing completion.

2.5 Other commitments

Particulars of all other material binding commitments should also be disclosed. This may include, for example, operating leases for equipment or premises used by the Church.

2.6 Loan liabilities secured on the PCC's assets

If any specific assets (whether land or other property) of the PCC are subject to a mortgage or charge, given as security for a loan or other liability, a note to the financial statements should disclose (a) particulars of the assets which are subject to the mortgage or charge, and (b) the amount of the loan or liability and its proportion of the present value of the assets mortgaged or charged.

2.7 Contingent liabilities

A contingency existing at the year-end which as a result of some probable future event is considered likely to crystallise into a material liability should cease to be contingent and should be accrued in the financial statements. The amount of the liability should be capable of being estimated with reasonable accuracy at the date on which the financial statements are approved.

The notes should disclose the nature of each contingency, the uncertainties that are expected to affect the outcome and a prudent estimate of the financial effect where an amount has not been accrued in the financial statements.

If such an estimate cannot be made, the financial statements should show why it is not practicable to make such an estimate.

2.8 Grants payable

If a PCC makes grants to institutions that are material in the context of its grant making, the PCC should disclose details of a sufficient number of these grants to provide an understanding of what the PCC has supported. The information given should include not only the purpose (or class of purpose), but also (subject to the exceptions, mentioned below), the name of the institution and total value of grants given.

The Trustees Annual Report should include the PCC's policy for making grants and show the nature of the institution receiving them.

There is no requirement to disclose any grants if they are not material in relation to the PCC's total expenditure, but PCCs will usually wish to disclose all their major contributions to other charitable bodies, whatever their value and this is to be encouraged. These can be shown in the annual report or in the notes to the financial statements (see note 3a to the example accrual accounts in Appendix ii). Very exceptionally the disclosure of details of grants made to institutions could seriously prejudice the purposes of either the PCC or the recipient. The Charities SORP (paragraph 209) explains what to do in these circumstances, by saying so in the notes and by giving the sensitive information to the Charity Commission on a confidential basis.

An unconditional or 'blanket' exception in s.132 of the Act provides that no disclosure need be made of the amount or the name of the recipient of any individual grant made out of a trust fund during the lifetime of its founder or spouse or civil partner. The only disclosures then required in the accounts notes are of the total amount of all such grants made in the year out of that trust fund and of their purpose(s).

2.9 Transactions with members of the PCC and related parties

Where a PCC enters into any material transaction, contract or other arrangement (including a grant or donation) with any related party, the amounts involved and the terms and conditions should be disclosed in the notes to the financial statements. Certain transactions need not be disclosed. These include donations of any money or in kind from PCC members or those closely connected with them (as long as any terms of trust imposed cannot be seen as altering materially the way the PCC operates), benefice property maintenance and employee contracts. These are unlikely to influence the separate independent interests of the charity. The total remuneration of employees is disclosed separately (see paragraph 2.10).

Any decision by the PCC to enter into a transaction should be, and should be seen to be, influenced only by the consideration of the Council's own interests as a charity. This is reinforced by charity law rules which, in certain circumstances, can invalidate transactions where the PCC has a conflict of interest. Therefore transactions with related parties (such as PCC members, their spouses and organisations connected with them) need to be disclosed. Transparency is particularly important where the relationship between the PCC and the other party or parties to a transaction suggests that the transaction could possibly have been influenced by interests other than the PCC's. It is possible, subject to charity law constraints, that the reported financial position and results may have been unlawfully affected by such transactions and 'to show that this has not happened' information about these transactions and their propriety is therefore necessary for readers of the PCC's financial statements.

Contracts or similar arrangements directly or indirectly involving PCC members personally or persons with a close family or business connection with them should always be regarded as material and the amounts involved, together with the name of the PCC member, disclosed in the notes. Any 'private benefit' element must be separately disclosed together with the legal authority for such benefit. This includes details of the total salary costs where a PCC member is also a PCC employee. Where the members have received no such remuneration or other taxable benefits, this fact should be stated.

Where travelling, subsistence or any other out-of-pocket expenses have been reimbursed to a member of the PCC or to a third party; the aggregate amount of all such expenses reimbursed should be disclosed in a note to the financial statements. The note should also indicate the nature of the expenses (e.g. travel, subsistence, entertainment etc.) and how many of the members have been reimbursed for the year. Where the members have received no such reimbursement, this fact should be stated.

Sometimes PCC members act as agents for the PCC and make approved purchases on its behalf and are reimbursed for this expenditure, e.g. payment for stationery or candles. Such reimbursed expenditure is not personal to the trustee concerned, nor does it count as goods or services provided by a PCC member personally, and as it is not a personal expense there is no need to disclose it. Likewise there is no need to disclose routine expenditure that is attributable collectively to the services provided by the PCC, such as providing reasonable refreshment for everyone at a PCC meeting.

2.10 Employee emoluments

The total staff costs showing the split between gross wages and salaries, employer's national insurance costs and pension costs and the average number of employees for the year, should be disclosed in the notes to the financial statements. Clergy paid through the diocese are not PCC employees.

If a PCC is over the audit threshold then the notes should also show the number of employees (if any) whose emoluments for the year fell within each band of £10,000 from £60,000 upwards.

2.11 Auditor's or independent examiner's remuneration

The notes to the financial statements should disclose separately the amount payable to the auditor or independent examiner in respect of:

(a)   audit or independent examination services; and

(b)   other financial services such as taxation advice, consultancy, financial advice and accountancy, disclosing the fees separately under each head.

2.12 Ex gratia payments

The total amount or value of any:

(a)   payment made; or

(b)   non-monetary benefit given; or

(c)   other expenditure of any kind; or

(d)   waiver of rights to property to which a PCC is entitled

which is made not as an application of funds or property for the general purposes of the PCC but in fulfilment of a compelling moral obligation, e.g. voluntarily surrendering part of a legacy if the reasonable needs of the testator's close family were not adequately provided for, should be disclosed in the notes to the financial statements. It should be noted that special authorisation is needed for a proposed 'ex gratia payment' and requires prior application to the Charity Commission, but that this does not normally include staff benefits of any kind.

2.13 Support costs

For the vast majority of PCCs support costs will be for church running expenses and there will be no need to allocate them across different expenditure categories. For PCCs above the audit threshold, however, support costs must be allocated to the relevant activity cost categories they support.

Support costs are those incurred in undertaking an activity that, while necessary to deliver an activity, do not themselves produce or constitute the output of the charitable activity. Similarly, costs will be incurred in supporting income generating activities such as fundraising, and in supporting the governance of the charity. They include generic costs such as payroll administration, accounting costs and computer maintenance. Since they do not constitute an activity but instead enable activities to be undertaken, they are allocated to the relevant activity cost category they support according to the following principles:

●   Where appropriate expenditure should be allocated directly to an activity cost category

- Items of expenditure which contribute directly to more than one activity cost category should be apportioned on a reasonable, justifiable and consistent basis e.g. the cost of a staff member whose time is divided between a fund-raising activity and a charitable activity should be apportioned on the basis of time spent on the particular activities.

There are a number of bases for apportionment that may be applied. Examples include:

- Usage e.g. electricity costs for the Church and the Hall

- Per capita

- Floor area

- Time

There should be a note to the financial statements that provides details of the total support costs incurred. If there are material items or categories of expenditure within this total these should be separately identified. It is recommended that a grid is used that lists the activities and the separately identifiable material support costs that have been allocated. If support costs are material, an explanation of how these costs have been allocated to each of the activity cost categories, i.e. the allocation basis, should be provided in the notes.

chapter 3

Principles of Trust Fund Accounting

What money should the PCC account for?

3.1 Responsibility

It is clear that the PCC should account in full for its incoming resources and for the way those resources are expended, but in many parishes it is not easy to identify just what the PCC is legally responsible for.

One of the principles of the charity accounting regime is that the charity trustees (here, the PCC members) should identify and include in their annual financial statements any resources that form part of their charity under ecclesiastical or trust law or which it controls and can benefit from.

The following are examples of situations that might arise. What are being described are organisations that may be connected with the Church and whose funds may be under the control of the PCC to its own benefit in some way:

- The PCC may have parochial organisations (such as a men's group, a mothers and toddlers group, or a Church Hall Management Committee) that operate as a part of the local church and are not controlled by another body (such as the Mothers' Union or the Girl Guides). The members may pay contributions which are used to cover the cost of meetings, refreshments, duplicating and speakers' expenses. The organisation may make a contribution to the PCC for the use of a meeting room or for the cost of heating and lighting.

- The PCC may also have funds belonging to it that are administered by members of the congregation, such as a flower fund to cover the cost of flowers in church or a choir fund with some of the money received for weddings.

- There may also be a 'Friends' organisation or a parochial trust to which parishioners are invited to contribute.

- There may also be various other trusts, perhaps with the incumbent and churchwardens as trustees and with the passage of time the control of the funds may have appeared to move to the PCC or the purpose of the funds may have become uncertain. (These may commonly be called 'Vicar and Wardens' trusts)

In all of these cases it is necessary to determine whether the income and costs belong to the PCC or to a separate charity or to a separate non-accountable body (e.g., a club or perhaps a 'corporation sole').

3.2 Tests that should be applied

To discover whether the funds of a particular organisation should be included within the PCC's financial statements, the following questions in the box should be addressed. These will test whether the activity is a special trust of the PCC or otherwise under its control. It may be that the PCC needs to make a public declaration about its legal responsibilities for particular parochial groups, organisations and activities. It is recommended that the PCC annually reviews, for accounting purposes, the list of all organisations for which it wishes to take responsibility or may be expected to take responsibility.

Is the PCC responsible? Questions to ask

Question 1

Is this group so constituted that it is in law a 'special trust' of the PCC? (A special trust in section 287 of the Charities Act 2011 is defined as 'assets which are held and administered by or on behalf of a charity for any special purposes of the charity, and is so held and administered on separate trusts relating only to that property').

–   If it is a special trust, then whoever is controlling it is normally accountable to the PCC and the PCC must include it in its financial statements. It will then be a restricted fund of the PCC. (See paragraph 3.9 for more information.)

–   If not, go to the next question.

Question 2

Does the PCC control the group? Related questions that may help to tease out the relationship concern whether the group has a separate constitution; whether it recognises the authority of the PCC or whether the group is a separate charitable institution. Using the Church's name and registration with HMRC for reclaiming tax brings it under the PCC's control but just using the Church's name in the group's title does not.

Question 3

Is the group under the control of some of the members of the PCC and are they acting as a subcommittee of the PCC in their control? If the PCC members outnumber the others in the control of the group, then the group is under the control of the PCC. The incumbent acting as a member of the PCC under its delegation may fulfil this function. For example, if the incumbent can restructure the control of the group, it is then appropriate to ask whether the incumbent is acting (i) in his/her own right or (ii) on behalf of the PCC. (It should be noted that the incumbent may be three bodies in one, with different capacities: acting in his/her own right as a person; acting alone as a 'corporation sole'; or in a representative capacity acting as chair of the PCC.)

–   If (i), then it has been established that the group is not under the control of the full PCC.

If other PCC members are involved in controlling the group, the same question should be asked if they are acting (i) in their own right or ii) on behalf of the PCC as a delegated committee?

–   If (i), then the question must be asked whether both sides think it is a connected charity – it is going to be 'connected' only by having parallel, common or related objects *and* being administered either in common with the PCC or by common trustees.

–   If (ii), then you are back to the answer to Question 2.

3.3   Applying the tests in practice

The following are examples of conclusions drawn from applying the tests:

● Funds raised using the PCC's charitable status to reclaim tax must be included within the PCC's financial statements. This applies to activities, such as a Mission Gift Day, when the money will eventually be given away outside the parish.

● Monies collected by parochial activities, such as women's or men's groups that are not associated with a parent organisation and are not under the control of the PCC, need not be included. However, each organisation should be encouraged to account for its income to its members. If the PCC underwrites such activities (i.e. pays the bills if the organisers cannot) then they are within PCC control if the organisers cannot show otherwise – (e.g., that the PCC only guarantees their creditworthiness but does not make decisions for them or claim their assets as its own).

● Monies that are collected by parochial organisations that are associated with a third party parent organisation, such as the Mothers' Union, are not included. These sums will be dealt with as a part of the financial statements of that organisation and any contribution made to the PCC for the use of meeting rooms will be received and recorded by the PCC, probably as a donation or as income from the letting of facilities. Those organisations should be disclosed in the Annual Report, explaining their relationship as associated charities working with the PCC in some way.

● Monies, restricted either as to their use or to their purpose, that have historically been collected by and from members of the congregation. Usually these resources have been handled totally separately from the PCC accounts and the interest of the PCC treasurer is considered to be an intrusion. However they are, and should be accounted for as, restricted income of the PCC.

● A 'Friends' organisation that raises funds for the upkeep of the church buildings. If the organisation is a registered charity, it will normally (especially if the PCC is not registered) account separately and file its own returns to the Charity Commission, but it will need to be mentioned in the PCC's Annual Report as a connected charity. If it is treated as an excepted charity under the umbrella of the PCC, then it is a branch and its accounts should be included with the PCC's financial statements.

A 'Friends' or other charitable organisation that is not under the PCC's 'umbrella' might not have its own charity registration number. If it has exclusively charitable purposes and a gross income below the registration threshold (currently £5,000 a year) it is not required to register with the Commission but (if only to prove its charitable status) it should still have a written constitution and, like any other charity must prepare annual accounts and behave charitably. If its income is above the registration threshold then those managing it are in breach of charity law and should correct this by either registering as an autonomous charity or coming under the control of the PCC.

The PCC should not include in its own (entity*) financial statements the income or expenditure of a separately accountable, independent registered charity associated with the Church (possibly the 'Friends') – but the Charities SORP requires any material transactions between a related party and the PCC or any of its connected charities to be disclosed in the accounts notes. However, if the 'Friends' settle any PCC bills directly, that amounts to either 'donated services/facilities' or a grant to the PCC, which if accruals accounts are prepared will then need to be accounted for as an incoming resource and as an appropriate expenditure. (*This means as distinct from group consolidated accounts, which are mandatory under the Charities Act 2011 only for groups exceeding £500,000 gross income – see Chapter 7.)

The specific accounting policies for any significant categories of income should be explained on the accruals basis of accounting.

3.4   What are trusts?

A trust is a device in English common law to enable an appointed person or group of people to manage property (i.e. money and/or other assets) for a purpose specified by the trust's founder. The Trust Deed sets out how the trustees, of which there must normally be at least two, if individuals, to sign off any land transfers, shall manage or dispense the assets of the trust. Not all trusts are charitable. To be charitable the trust must have a purpose that is exclusively charitable in law and is for the public benefit.

There may be a variety of charitable trusts within the parish. In order to account correctly for these it will be necessary to identify and classify them. This may require some work depending on how carefully they have been administered in the past (although it should only need to be done once). However, accounting requirements apart, it is important to ensure that property held on trust is administered by the right trustees and used for the right purpose.

There may be some trusts which are not part of or connected with the PCC and which will be subject to the normal registration and accounting regimes as with any other charity. These could include:

● The trust of a Church school site and associated endowments held by trustees other than the PCC (e.g. the incumbent and churchwardens).

- Other educational trusts not held by the PCC. Some parishes have Sunday school or religious education funds created by orders under section 554 of the Education Act 1996 (previously section 2 of the Education Act 1973). These 'three-fourteenths' trusts arise from the proceeds of sale of former Church school sites. It was traditional for the incumbent to have use of the school for half Saturday and all Sunday – hence three-fourteenths – and the Church school used the premises for the rest of the time. When the school is closed, three-fourteenths can remain in the parish, normally under the trusteeship of the incumbent and churchwardens (which was the traditional pattern for Church school trusteeship). The trust, if it has an income over £5,000, will normally have to be registered in its own right and publicly accounted for by its trustees under the normal charity accounting rules. It is not 'a hidden pot of gold' which can be appropriated for the PCC's general purposes.

- Other incumbent and churchwardens trusts will also be separate charities unless they are special trusts of the PCC (see paragraph 3.5).

Then there will be charitable trusts which are or may be connected with the PCC. They may simply have to be accounted for as one of the three main types of PCC fund, but it may be that they need to be 'tidied up' first to clarify what they are for, or that something can be done to make their administration more straightforward. Trusts in this category may be special trusts or they may be controlled charities of the PCC. The former are trusts of property held and administered by or on behalf of the PCC on separate trusts for any special purposes of the PCC:

- the property must be held on separate trusts (as could arise with a gift or legacy);

- it must be held and administered by or on behalf of the PCC, and so the trustees may not necessarily be the PCC itself;

- it must be held for a special purpose of the PCC and so a mere coincidence of objects is not sufficient – the trust must be for a part of the purpose of the PCC.

Therefore a trust held by the incumbent and churchwardens for general ecclesiastical purposes in the parish would not be a special trust of the PCC even though the PCC could also use its general funds for these purposes, but a trust held by the incumbent and churchwardens for the express purpose of assisting the PCC in the maintenance of the churchyard would be a special trust of the PCC.

Sometimes, after carrying out all reasonable investigations, it will prove difficult or impossible to classify a particular trust or fund. If the amount involved is large it may be necessary to involve professional advisers to clarify the terms of the trust. However, if the amount is small so that the cost of unravelling the trust terms would be out of proportion to the value of its assets, parishes may wish to adopt a common sense approach and account for the trust as a special trust of the PCC or a controlled 'charity-branch', so that at least it is accounted for somewhere.

3.5 Special trusts

A special trust in section 287 of the Charities Act 2011 is defined as 'assets which are held and administered by or on behalf of a charity for any special purposes of the charity, and is so held and administered on separate trusts relating only to that property'.

3.6 Incumbent and churchwardens' trusts

Trusts where the incumbent and churchwardens are trustees generally fall into three categories:

Trusts for ecclesiastical purposes
(e.g. maintenance of the church and churchyard): these are already required to be vested in the Diocesan Board of Finance (DBF) as custodian trustee. They will have similar objects to those of the PCC and will be included in the PCC's accounts.

Trusts for educational purposes
(e.g. Sunday school funds arising from the sale of a Church school): these are registered with the Department for Education. They are entirely separate from the PCC's financial statements, however there may be cases where as 'connected charities' the existence of such charities is disclosable in

the PCC's Annual Report, describing the relationship (e.g., the vicar is on both boards, etc.) for the information of parishioners.

Trusts for the relief of poverty
(e.g. to provide food or clothing for poor people in the parish): unless they are very small these should already be registered with the Charity Commission. Again, they are entirely separate from the PCC's financial statements, however there may be cases where as 'connected charities' the existence of such charities is disclosable in the PCC's Annual Report, describing the relationship (e.g., the vicar is on both boards, etc.) for the information of parishioners.

These trusts will normally need to be shown as a part of the PCC's financial statements. In exceptional circumstances they will need to be disclosed as 'connected charities' in the PCC's Annual Report and the relationship explained – in terms of any trustees and purposes in common and how the trust's activities dovetail with those of the PCC.

It should be noted that where incumbents and churchwardens, as the charity trustees of these trusts, have a legal responsibility to account publicly for them, any member of the public can ask for a copy of the statutory financial statements of such trusts.

How should the PCC account for its funds?

This section describes the nature of the different funds the PCC will hold so that they can be separated in the records and the financial statements to demonstrate that the PCC has observed the specific terms of trust attaching to those funds.

3.7 Funds

The PCC may allocate certain sums of money to particular funds for particular purposes or it may raise funds for particular purposes. The following are examples of the names of some of these funds which may have grown up over the years:

General Fund	Bell Fund
Church Restoration Fund	Choir & Organ Fund
Church Hall Fund	Legacies Fund
General Bequest Fund	Sunday School Fund
Building Fund	Mission & Charities Fund
Fabric Fund	Churchyard Fund
Flower Fund	Maintenance Reserve Fund

In addition there may be funds in the name of the person who gave or left the money, possibly for a particular purpose.

Each of these funds is associated with a particular purpose or, in the case of some legacies, with the source of the funds. But the fund names do not immediately tell the reader of the financial statements whether they are held by the PCC on trust for a restricted purpose.

The word 'fund' has an additional use in charity accounting. As well as referring to money allocated by the PCC itself out of its general-purpose funds to be set aside for a particular use (e.g. fixed assets needed for the PCC to function) or project (e.g. to fund the provision of childcare or visits to special-needs parishioners), it is also used where the money is restricted in some way by the donor or by the terms of an appeal. With this latter meaning, each such fund is restricted by trust law, being either income that must be spent only on a specified purpose or else being capital (endowment) in nature that must be retained for the PCC's own use or for investment. In the latter case the investment income may or may not be restricted to spending on a specified purpose. It is important to know the difference between these types of fund as PCCs have to observe clear distinctions between them.

As stated above, many PCCs will already distinguish between all their funds by reference to the purpose to which they have been earmarked (such as those in the list above) or else restricted by law. For some, a clarification will be needed to record properly whether the fund is restricted (and if so, whether it is endowed) and for what purpose, or else unrestricted (and, if so, to confirm its status if designated for a particular purpose) in order to be able to demonstrate that the PCC has properly exercised the trust placed in it.

The charity accounting framework requires fund-based financial statements that in any case enable the reader to see that the PCC is spending its funds on the purposes for which they have been given. It may be helpful for smaller PCCs to give the project-based information, which is not required by law below the statutory audit threshold, as well as the funding aspect – i.e., surplus or deficit, either in a note to the financial statements or in the annual report (e.g. 'sales of the parish magazine exceeded printing costs by £140'). Even if not given in the financial statements, such information is likely to be important for the PCC in carrying out its responsibilities, and thus it may be appropriate to report such information in the 'Performance and Achievements' section of the annual report.

3.8 Unrestricted funds

All PCCs have a general-purpose income fund, normally called a General Fund, which they use to pay all the everyday expenses. This fund is 'unrestricted' because the money has been given to the Church on the general understanding that it will be used at the discretion of the PCC for furthering the mission and ministry of the Church. Unless specified otherwise, all the money received by the Church is put into the General Fund. Income generated from assets held in an unrestricted fund will be unrestricted income.

The PCC may decide to put some of the unrestricted fund money aside in other funds for use in the future (for example, for future building repairs). This money is 'designated' for these particular projects for administration purposes only. Designated funds are still unrestricted and can be moved to other general funds (re-designated or un-designated) if the PCC so decides. It is also important to bear in mind that these designated funds cannot at any time exceed the total amount of the General Fund – i.e., you cannot earmark money for future spending before you get it, so they cannot leave you with a negative figure for the General Fund's 'free reserves' (i.e., undesignated monies) but must be capped if necessary to avoid that. This is important because of the requirement to disclose in the Annual Report the trustees' policy on reserves, the actual reserves level at the year-end what is being done to bridge any gap between the aimed-for and actual levels of free reserves.

3.9 Restricted funds

PCCs also receive money which has been given for a particular purpose, for example:

(i)   a collection in church may be announced as being for a particular purpose (such as the purchase of new hymn books, or the repair of the tower);

(ii) a fund-raising event (such as a rummage sale or a coffee morning) may be held for a particular purpose;

(iii) a donation may have been made or a legacy may have been left to the church for a particular purpose (such as the upkeep of the churchyard or the repair of the fabric).

All these sums have been restricted by the donor for a particular purpose and unless the donor has specifically reserved a right of consent to variation of purpose they cannot, and must not, be used by the PCC for any other purpose unless determined by the courts or the Charity Commission or else, for small trusts, the purpose is varied under the statutory powers given to trustees in the 2011 Act. Income generated from assets held in a restricted fund will generally be subject to the same restrictions as the fund the asset belongs to (unless the donor has specified otherwise).

An oral or written appeal or a collection for a special purpose, such as the fabric fund, will restrict the income to that purpose. There may be times when more money is raised than is needed for the particular purpose of the appeal. This excess money is restricted to the purpose and should be retained for use for the same purpose, or returned to the donors (except under the Gift Aid Scheme, which prohibits refunds).

This situation can be eased if the PCC acquires the power beforehand to use any surpluses for other purposes. The easiest way to avoid any problem is by announcing at the time of the appeal that any unused balance will be put to the general purposes of the PCC unless a donor explicitly forbids this (which would be a rarity). The restriction then applies until the purpose of the appeal has been satisfied. (A general notice to this effect can be placed prominently in the church to catch all occasions.) If someone wants to make a significant donation for a particular purpose, the donor could be invited to specify that they give the PCC permission to use it or a surplus for general or alternative specific purposes under certain conditions.

There could also be a potential problem if insufficient funds are raised for a particular purpose and the shortfall cannot be made good out of general funds. The PCC should always make clear in appeals what it would do if this situation were to lead to the project being abandoned – for example, to return all the donations (except where this is prohibited under the Gift Aid rules) or to use them for another related purpose.

When special collections are made to send straight off to other charities (e.g. Christian Aid, missionary societies) and the nature of the appeal is that there is no discretion for the PCC to do anything other than send the money directly to the charity, these are not funds of the PCC, as it is acting only as a collecting agent, and so the appeal should not be included in the PCC's gross income or total expenditure. It is good practice to include a list of these collections in the PCC's Annual Report, if only to confirm to the congregation that all appeals money collected has been duly passed on to the intended charity.

3.10 Endowment funds

Another form of restricted fund is known as an endowment. This is either capital money given to the Church as permanent or (alternatively) expendable* capital with the specific instruction that only the income gained from investing the money can be spent, or it is a capital asset (such as a house) donated to be retained for continuing use by the Church. (*If the donor has in any way authorised the spending of capital, it will be an 'expendable' endowment to the extent of the trustees' discretionary power to spend it.) The original money or assets (the 'capital') cannot be spent as income unless so authorised and must remain in the form of equivalent fixed assets (such as a house) or investments, but not necessarily the same asset that was given. It may be in a fund that is named after the donor.

There are thus two types of endowment capital, which must be distinguished in accruals accounts by note:

(i) **permanent:**
a particular type of restricted fund where the capital, in accordance with the explicit requirements of the founding donor, must be held permanently (the PCC have no power to convert any of it into income for spending like other income). Any income return generated by the invested endowment (e.g. dividends) should be spent as determined by the donor, whereas any investment holding or disposal gains (less losses) belong to capital on the same terms as the original gift.

(ii) **expendable:**
an endowment fund where the capital may, in certain circumstances, be spent. (The PCC have this power, if given by the donor. This fund is not income when it is first received because there is no duty on the part of the PCC to spend it for its intended purposes. The PCC has the legal right (and even the duty) to retain the capital as capital and a further legal right to convert capital into income in accordance with the express or implied terms of trust imposed by the donor. However, if the power to convert is used, then at that time the amount converted becomes income.) Any income return generated by the invested endowment will be required by law to be spent as determined by the donor without unreasonable delay and so cannot just be added to the retained capital unless a specific legal power to 'accumulate' income as capital allows this. Any investment holding or disposal gains (less losses) belong to capital on the same terms as the original gift.

Any expenses incurred in the administration of the capital fund (such as the fees of the person who manages the investments) should be charged against the capital of the fund unless the founding donor clearly intended otherwise. However, if the trust establishing a fund provides for it or if the capital fund has insufficient liquid assets to meet such costs (e.g. they cannot be used, as they consist only of land or buildings needed for the PCC's own use), the expenses can be charged to income (normally to the general fund).

3.11 Accounting for different types of fund

Where a PCC holds trust funds other than unrestricted funds, its accounting records must be adequate to allow separate accounts to be produced for each distinct trust fund. Restricted income funds and endowment capital funds must be shown separately in the annual financial statements. PCCs should also show in the accounts notes (if not in the balance sheet) how any designated funds have moved between year-ends.

In the accounting records this administrative separation to comply with trust law can be done either by using separate columns in the cash book for the different types of trust fund or by clearly labelling each entry to distinguish those that are unrestricted and those that are restricted as to capital or as to income or merely designated.

In the annual financial statements unrestricted, restricted and endowment funds must be reported separately. As a minimum all funds of one type should be reported together, either as three separate columns (see example in the Receipts and Payments Accounts section) or, in the case of accounts on the Receipts and Payments basis, alternatively as separate statements of account. It is important that the reader can tell that the funds are not all held on the same legal basis and it is important that the PCC members know that certain funds have restrictions on the way the money can be used. The PCC must also be able to demonstrate that it still holds assets belonging to restricted and endowment funds and has not used these for unauthorised spending, nor for unauthorised purposes. It is a breach of trust to spend restricted income funds for purposes other than those for which they were given without the prior consent of the Charity Commission, or to spend trust capital without proper authority.

The PCC's unused monies, unless held for immediate spending, may need to be invested and investment income generated. Any income earned belongs to the fund whose assets were invested and the income is subject to the same restrictions as that fund. Therefore, the investment income must be attributed to each fund, and in the case of investment pooling* this must be based on the amounts invested by each fund and the time for which they were invested, and must be accounted for as part of the fund to which they belonged. (*Statutory authority for this is provided by the Trustee Act 2000.)

The only exceptions to this are:

(i)   where the donor has expressly provided for some other use for the income;

(ii)   where the asset is part of a permanent endowment held for general purposes. In this case the capital is restricted in an endowment fund (because it cannot be spent) but the income is unrestricted since it can be spent for the PCC's general purposes or for any designated purpose.

If an endowment fund has assets (e.g. a house or investments) and any are sold, the proceeds of sale must be held within the same endowment fund. The same applies to the sale of investment securities belonging to a restricted income fund.

SORP 2005 makes it clear that funds may be grouped and sub-analysed by major fund in the notes to the financial statements, and so all endowments may be reported on as one group, all other restricted funds as another group and all funds with no restriction as a third group.

In some cases, other bodies of trustees may hold funds from which the PCC is legally entitled to benefit. If such trustees are only the custodians (i.e. they have no discretion over the use of the fund) then that money is a fund (in most cases an endowment fund) of the PCC. If the PCC does not have enough discretion over the use of funds held in its name to make it the 'charity trustee' of those funds, then they should not be accounted for in the PCC's financial statements. Instead, the fact of the fund's existence, its purpose and a description of the assets belonging to it should be disclosed in the PCC's Annual Report together with how the connected charity's activity relates to that of the PCC and how the necessary segregation of assets is maintained.

With parishes bearing an increasingly larger part of the costs of maintaining the Church of England it may seem odd to think that there may be parishes who have received income which they may find difficult to spend. Usually these will relate to restricted funds. Some examples might include the following:

● The PCC has investments in a restricted fund which are the proceeds of a house used for curates and parish staff in the past. This may be from a period in between employment of one staff member and another when a house has been bought in which it is possible that the parish is subsequently not required to house a worker; the PCC will then have to consider what to do with the fund.

● A building appeal fund has been set up but because the proper permissions have not yet been granted there is some doubt whether the project will go ahead.

● Money has been specifically raised to send an individual to do a specific project in a third world country but because of a recent civil war that person cannot go or that project is stalled.

The status of such funds should be explained in the notes to the financial statements and any proposed action to dispose of the unexpended balances should be disclosed. This may include returning funds to the donors (subject to Gift Aid Scheme rules), or obtaining permission (either from the donors (if, unusually, they had reserved to themselves a power of variation of the terms of trust) or by order of the Charity Commission) for the funds to be spent on other purposes.

Tips for handling different funds

● Clear records of restricted money should be kept so that it can readily be identified. Poor records can lead to confused administration and then it is possible that the rules will be ignored and restricted and unrestricted funds will be unlawfully merged with one another.

● Expenditure of restricted funds may anticipate promised funding at the time the expenditure is incurred. It is acceptable practice in such cases to show a deficit on the project and then wait for the promised funding before deciding what balance must be met from the general fund. However, any insufficiency of the general fund for this purpose cannot be made good out of other restricted funds. Where material, deficit balances on restricted funds should be shown separately on the face of the balance sheet, and not netted off against other restricted fund balances. Details will also need to be given in the Annual Report (see Chapter 6).

● Collections at some funerals are taken in a bowl by the church door and are taken by the undertaker for a specific purpose at the wish of the bereaved family. These collections should only be recorded and accounted for by the PCC if the money is given directly to the Church or the PCC makes the decision as to the use to which it should be put.

● Fees for the services of bell ringers, organists, vergers or choir at weddings and for organists, vergers and gravediggers at funerals and fees belonging to the diocesan board of finance, need not be included in the financial statements if the money is paid over in full directly to those involved. In this case the PCC is acting as an intermediary and these fees do not count towards PCC income. PCCs will from time to time collect money on behalf of other charities in a public place or in church services. Examples of this include Christmas carolling and Christian Aid door-to-door collections. In these instances these receipts are not to be included in the PCC's income as the PCC is acting as an agent for the charity. This is the case whether the money collected is sent off to the charity or if the money is counted and the PCC treasurer writes out a cheque for money paid into its bank account.

● PCCs should remember that they do not have to accept a gift if they are uncertain of its source or if they are not happy at abiding by the donor's conditions. All gifts for which the PCC reclaims tax under the Gift Aid scheme must be shown in the financial statements and its use agreed by the PCC. This would include the situation where tax is reclaimed on a donation paid by Gift Aid to be used for the PCC's charitable purposes at the minister's discretion.

● There is no formal reason why PCCs should agree to accept every gift but written evidence of gifts and their restrictions should be obtained wherever possible.

● Legacies given for the general purposes of the PCC should immediately be credited to the general fund. Unless the donor has restricted the use of the legacy in the Will, it remains unrestricted and may not be restricted by the PCC. All or a part of the legacy may then be designated for a particular purpose but it should not be designated to a 'Legacy Fund' with no intention as to its use.

- The separate administration of differently restricted funds does not require them necessarily to be kept in separate bank accounts, but this may be a useful practice in some circumstances as it does guarantee that they can always be identified as such.

- In the past, many parishes have operated with a large number of funds for different aspects of the Church's life. Such a large number involves administrative complexity in the accounting system and the published financial statements. PCCs are recommended to keep under review the number of funds while taking care not to conflict with the strict rules on restricted and endowment funds.

- PCCs are advised to ensure that they have proper systems in place for the signing of cheques, the counting of collections (including the opening of planned giving envelopes) and their prompt payment into the bank. Charity Commission leaflet CC8 provides useful information.

Tips for handling other church funds

- The treasurer (on behalf of the PCC) should ensure that proper accounting records are kept by PCC 'branches' (organisations and those who hold the purses for small extra funds for which the PCC is accountable in law). Each year the treasurer will need to obtain an accurate return from each 'branch', which can be quite simple, consisting of a summary of Receipts and Payments for the year, and a list of any assets and liabilities at the year-end. The figures from these organisations or funds should be added to the PCC's financial statements if they are material.

- Unless these 'branches' are a separately accountable legal entity, all the funds that they hold are the legal property of the PCC, whether or not they have a separate bank account.

- 'Friends' organisations not under the control of the PCC should be advised to have themselves properly constituted.

- There are other important reasons for establishing the status of Church organisations, such as concerns over insurance cover and responsibilities under the Children Act 1989.

- From 1 January 2013, a portion of the parochial fees received becomes the legal property of the Diocesan Board of Finance (under the Ecclesiastical Fees (Amendment) Measure 2011) with the remaining portion belonging to the PCC. These are separate fees: one forms part of the PCC's income while the other is the DBF's income (unless the fees are not assigned, when they will continue to be declared by the freehold incumbent whose stipend is reduced accordingly). It is therefore important that, when one cheque is received for both types of fee, the treasurer ensures that the relevant portion is paid to the DBF. Guidance to the new Measure strongly suggests that in all cases (other than for non-assigned freeholders) incumbents should not handle fees, but that the PCC should be the local agent. The treasurer should not include the DBF's fee as part of PCC income in any way because they are only acting as an agent for the DBF when they collect fees on the DBF's behalf.

chapter 4

Statement of Financial Activities (SOFA)

What money should the PCC account for?

This chapter lists the various incoming and outgoing resources for which PCCs may be responsible, and collates them under the activity headings which are statutory for PCCs which are over the audit threshold. The recommended categories follow on from the receipts and payments categories, although there are some major differences arising, principally concerned with the treatment of fixed assets and of any gifts-in-kind of assets or services, i.e., their recognition at monetary value, and the depreciation of fixed assets in use by the PCC, and also of course the requirement for any auditable charity to categorise its expenditure on activities by reference to their purpose rather than the nature of the expense.

4.1 Format

The SOFA should summarise for the year all incoming resources of the PCC, both capital (endowment) and income, and all resources expended by it, analysed in accordance with their nature or by activity and across the different categories of funds. It should also reconcile all movements in the funds since the previous 31 December.

An example SOFA is shown below. The SOFA should be supported by notes. A full example, including notes summarising the movements in significant individual funds, is shown in Appendix ii.

SORP 2005 requires that charities over the audit threshold should analyse their incoming resources and resources expended by activity according to the purpose of that activity. The SORP also provides (appendix 5.3) that charities below the audit threshold may use any analysis of incoming and outgoing resources that may be best suited to their circumstances. This chapter sets out how PCCs can group their incoming resources and resources expended into the SORP's purpose-based categories and it is recommended that PCCs should, as far as possible, follow this approved layout as this has been designed to cover most of the PCC's activities and sources of funding. This layout will also provide the information needed to complete the annual return of parish finance.

Headings may be omitted where there is nothing to report in both the current and preceding years.

Within the two separate sections of 'incoming resources' and 'resources expended', the individual sub-headings may be changed in order to present a true and fair view of the PCC's activities.

Example Statement of Financial Activities

PAROCHIAL CHURCH COUNCIL OF ST LEDGER, AMBRIDGE

STATEMENT OF FINANCIAL ACTIVITIES

For the year ending 31 December 2012

	Note	Unrestricted Funds £	Restricted Funds £	Endowment Funds £	TOTAL 2012 £	TOTAL 2011 £
INCOMING RESOURCES						
Voluntary income	2(a)	160,400	216,750	-	377,150	148,750
Activities for generating funds	2(b)	10,000	-	-	10,000	4,250
Income from investments	2(c)	7,450	2,500	-	9,950	8,800
Church activities	2(d)	15,800	-	-	15,800	13,150
TOTAL INCOMING RESOURCES		193,650	219,250	-	412,900	174,950
RESOURCES EXPENDED						
Church activities	3(a)	154,300	244,275	-	398,575	161,275
Cost of generating voluntary income	3(b)	550	1,250	-	1,800	500
Governance Costs	3(c)	950	-	-	950	675
TOTAL RESOURCES EXPENDED		155,800	245,525	-	401,325	162,450
NET INCOMING RESOURCES BEFORE TRANSFERS		37,850	(26,275)	-	11,575	12,500
GROSS TRANSFERS BETWEEN FUNDS	5	(19,000)	19,000	-	-	-
NET INCOMING RESOURCES BEFORE OTHER RECOGNISED GAINS AND LOSSES		18,850	(7,275)	-	11,575	12,500
OTHER RECOGNISED GAINS:						
Gains on investment assets	6(b) & 7(a)	5,455	1,050	245	6,750	500
NET MOVEMENT IN FUNDS		24,305	(6,225)	245	18,325	13,000
Balances b/fwd 1 January 2012	9	58,935	14,000	2,250	75,185	62,185
Balances c/fwd 31 December 2012	10	83,240	7,775	2,495	93,510	75,185

The notes on pages 3 to 7 form part of this account.

4.2 Incoming resources

All incoming resources becoming available to the PCC during the year must be summarised in the SOFA, distinguishing between those belonging to its unrestricted funds, its restricted income funds and its endowment capital funds. These should be classified in accordance with the activity headings set out in this chapter, namely:

> Voluntary income
>
> Activities for generating funds
>
> Investment income
>
> Church activities
>
> Other incoming resources

These comprise the total incoming resources, but do not necessarily equate to the 'gross income' (see Chapter 1, sections 1.3 and 1.4).

In the notes to the financial statements, endowment fund incoming resources should be analysed between permanent endowment and expendable endowment.

The SOFA should enable the reader of the financial statements to gain an accurate appreciation of the principal elements of the incoming resources of the charity, but should not be excessively detailed. Supporting analyses should be provided in notes to the financial statements.

4.3 Resources expended

All resources expended should be included in the SOFA in the year in which they are incurred.

The resources expended section of the SOFA should distinguish between various types of expenditure in a way that is appropriate to the PCC's activities, and between fund types (with supplementary analysis of any individual major funds by way of note). For PCCs above and below the audit threshold, the Church's recommended activity classifications to be adopted are namely:

> Church activities
>
> Costs of generating funds
>
> Governance costs
>
> Other resources expended

4.4 Transfers between funds

Each column in the SOFA should be totalled to show the net incoming/outgoing resources before transfers. If the PCC has restricted income funds or endowment funds, or if designated funds are shown separately in the SOFA, any transfers between funds should be shown as a separate line. Material transfers between the different classes of funds should not be netted off, but should be shown gross, with supporting explanations in the notes. Transfers should, of course, net off to zero in the total column.

4.5 Net incoming resources for the year

Each column should again be totalled to give 'Net incoming resources before other recognised gains and losses'. Other recognised gains and losses relate to the re-valuations of both functional fixed assets and investment assets, but they relate to disposals only in the case of investment assets. These gains should be recorded as part of the fund in which the relevant asset is or was held. The following categories should be recorded on separate lines:

(a) revaluation (for disposals see 4.16) gains and losses on fixed assets held for the PCC's own use (for example, a curate's house);

(b) gains and losses on investment assets (i) sold in the year and those (ii) revalued at the year end.

It is not necessary to split the investment gain between realized and unrealized categories.

Each column of the Statement will then be totalled to show the net movement in funds of the PCC for the year as shown in the example above.

4.6 Reconciliation of funds

To the net movement in funds for the year for each column should be added the total funds brought forward from the previous balance sheet, to show the amounts of the total funds carried forward as shown in the balance sheet at the year-end.

4.7 Comparative figures

In the SOFA, corresponding amounts for the previous year are required only in total for all funds on each line, but it may help the reader if it is shown fund by fund wherever separate supporting movement statements are provided elsewhere (i.e. by way of note) for any of the underlying funds.

Accounting for incoming resources

4.8 Recognition in the Statement of Financial Activities

Members of the PCC have a legal duty to take reasonable care that everything they are entrusted with is properly applied, which in the first place means safeguarding everything to which the PCC becomes entitled as soon as this entitlement becomes legally enforceable. This includes not only actual receipts of the year but also any money or other property – whatever its source or purpose – which could have been received if the PCC had exercised its legal right to take possession of it. It should be accounted for as incoming resources of the PCC for the year.

The value of all resources – both for income and endowment funds – accruing to the PCC should be recorded in the Statement of Financial Activities as soon as it is practicable to do so. In all cases incoming resources should be recognised as and when the following three accounting requirements are met:

(a) entitlement – normally arises when a particular resource is receivable or the PCC's right to it becomes legally enforceable (unless its utilisation by the PCC has been deferred by the donor);

(b) certainty – when there is reasonable certainty that the incoming resource will ultimately be received;

(c) measurement – when the monetary value of the incoming resource can be measured with sufficient reliability.

4.9 Gifts in kind

Where material these should be included within 'Incoming resources' in the SOFA as follows:

(a) Assets given for use by the PCC, e.g. photocopier for use in the church office, should be recognised as incoming resources when receivable.

(b) Where a gift has been made in kind but on trust for conversion into cash and subsequent application by the PCC, the incoming resource should normally be recognised in the accounting period when receivable; but in certain cases this will not be practicable. In these cases the income should be included in the accounting period in which the gift is sold.

In all cases the amount at which gifts in kind are brought into account should be either a reasonable estimate of their value to the PCC or the amount actually realised. The basis of any valuation should be disclosed. Where material, an adjustment should be made to the original valuation upon subsequent realisation of the gift.

4.10 Donated services and facilities

A PCC may receive assistance in the form of donated facilities, beneficial loan arrangements, donated services (such as the provision of office accommodation where the rental is paid by a third party or the free use of telephone facilities) or services from volunteers. Such incoming resources should only be included in the SOFA where the benefit to the PCC is reasonably quantifiable and measurable. Donated services and facilities include those normally provided by an individual or entity as part of their trade or profession for a fee, but will exclude the value of contribution from volunteers as their contribution cannot be reasonably quantified in financial terms. The cost in the SOFA should be the estimated value to the PCC of the service or facility received. This will be the price the PCC estimates it would pay in the open market for a service or facility of equivalent utility to the PCC. An equivalent amount should be included in the SOFA as expenditure under the appropriate heading. As a result, both the value of this incoming resource and its contribution to the application of resources is recognised.

Most PCCs receive substantial amounts of voluntary help. Such help should not be accounted for in the SOFA, but should be gratefully acknowledged in the annual report, where it can also be quantified.

4.11 Donor-imposed restrictions

Where money is given to the PCC specifically to provide a fixed asset or where a fixed asset is donated (a gift in kind), the PCC will normally have entitlement to ownership and use of the gift at the point when it is receivable. At this point, the gift should be recognised in the SOFA and not deferred over the life of the asset. The possibility of having to repay the gift does not affect their recognition in the first place. Once acquired, the use of the asset will be either restricted or unrestricted. If the use is restricted the asset will be held in a restricted fund (as an endowment, to reflect the donor's intention of 'continuing' use). If its retention and use are unrestricted (i.e. the PCC is free to sell the asset and spend the proceeds for general purposes) the trustees may consider creating a designated fund to 'ring fence' its carrying value from the PCC's 'free' reserves. The relevant fund (endowment or designated) should then be reduced over the useful economic life of the asset in line with its depreciation.

When a PCC receives a gift, bequest or grant it will account for it, in either an unrestricted or restricted fund, once it is entitled to it and there are no pre-conditions preventing its use. A condition which prevents entitlement and use must be one that is outside the PCC's control (such as obtaining offers of matched funding from a third party or that the funds may only be expended in a later accounting period). When such a condition applies, the receipt should not be included in the SOFA until the pre-condition has been met (i.e. until the money can lawfully be spent). The amount of such 'deferred income' will instead be shown in the balance sheet as a 'liability'. The financial statements notes should explain all movements in 'deferred income', to enable the reader to understand the implications.

4.12 Accounting for tax recoverable under the Gift Aid Scheme

By the end of the year the PCC is likely to have received voluntary income on which tax can be reclaimed under the GiftAid Scheme. The tax claim for the year must be recognised in the financial statements in full within the fund to which the donation belongs, namely:

- any amounts that have been claimed and received from HMRC that relate to donations made to the PCC during the year; and

- any amounts that have been claimed from HMRC but not yet received; and

- any amounts that could have yet to be claimed at the year-end ('claimable').

Tax repayable to the PCC should be included in the SOFA in the same year as the income to which it relates, and even if disclosed separately as shown in the example, must be credited to the fund it belongs to – as stated above. Any such tax claim not received at the end of the year should be accounted for as a debtor until the PCC receives payment from HMRC.

4.13 Legacies

Legacies receivable should be included in the SOFA in accordance with the general principles for the recognition of incoming resources. They should not be included until it is reasonably certain that they will be received and the amount can be measured with sufficient reliability.

Where the PCC is aware of an entitlement to a material legacy which for the above reason has not been included in the financial statements, this fact and an estimate of the amount receivable should be disclosed in the notes to the financial statements.

4.14 Grants receivable

Receipts by way of grant should be treated in a similar manner to other incoming resources. They should be dealt with in the SOFA in accordance with the terms of the grant. This means, for example, that grants intended for specific purposes should be accounted for as restricted funds – endowed or non-endowed as the case may be. Grants received as for ordinary activities of the PCC but which are then designated by the PCC to specific purposes should be included as receipts in unrestricted funds, and then shown in the SOFA as a transfer from unrestricted to designated funds.

Grants should not be recognised until the pre-conditions (if any) for their receipt and use have been met. Once these pre-conditions are met, the grant should be recognised in the SOFA even if (as is normally the case) the resources are received in advance of related expenditure or if there is a condition that all or part of the donation may be repaid to the donor in specified circumstances. If repayment is possible then, depending on the probability, it should be noted as a contingent liability or recognised as an actual liability.

4.15 Trading activities

Some churches carry on trading activities such as letting church premises, selling books, producing magazines and running community cafés. Some of these activities may be outside the PCC's objects and care should be taken with major trading activities in case it is appropriate to form a separate trading company for liability and tax reasons. All proceeds of trading should be recognised as income of the year in which the 'sale' took place and any associated costs should be included in expenditure at the same time. The accounting principles for the recognition of assets and of liabilities require all trading income to be recognised in the SOFA at the point where an asset of the PCC is created or liability settled (i.e., when the PCC makes the sale) and likewise all trading costs to be recognised in the SOFA at the point where the external liability arises or a reduction in PCC assets occurs (normally when goods are sold from stock or services purchased for fulfilment of a sale). Where goods are purchased in one year but not sold until a later year, they should be shown in the balance sheet as stocks, in current assets, and charged to expenditure when the sale takes place.

Trading which is part of the PCC's charitable objects to further the work of the church (such as income from hall letting for church purposes and the sale of religious books) should be separated from fund-raising trading (such as selling postcards and souvenirs to tourists).

Some 'trading' involves merely the disposal of gifts in kind donated to the church (such as cakes for a cake stall or clothing for a rummage sale). In economic terms these are similar to trading and the proceeds should be accounted for as activities for generating funds.

Even if the cost of the trading activity is immaterial it is not acceptable simply to show the net trading result (profit or loss) in the SOFA.

If more than one trading activity is undertaken, then each significant activity should be separately disclosed, but this can be done in the notes.

All forms of trading should be recognised in this manner if significant.

4.16 Disposal of fixed assets used for the functioning of the PCC

Any net gain arising on disposal of fixed assets (the sale proceeds less the book value) previously used by the PCC for its functional purposes (such as the curate's house or the office photocopier) should be included in the SOFA as an incoming resource of the fund concerned. If a net loss arises for the year, it should be included as an additional depreciation charge to the fund concerned under the appropriate heading of charitable or other expenditure. If material, the gains and losses should be disclosed separately, with a supporting note by way of explanation.

4.17 Netting off

All incoming resources should, as far as practicable, be reported gross and not netted off against expenditure. This means, for example, that expenditure on putting on a fund-raising event such as a fete should not be netted off against the funds raised. On occasions it may not be practicable to report the resources gross i.e., if the event is not under the control of the PCC and it's merely a passive beneficiary of the net proceeds raised. In such a case the reason for netting off should be given in the notes and an estimate of the gross funds raised and the deducted expenditure given in the SOFA.

4.18 Cost of generating funds

Voluntary income raised by the PCC should be brought into account gross, and associated costs should be accounted for as fund-raising expenditure.

4.19 Analysis

This list below is given as an aid and all the Account Descriptions which are used in keeping the accounts need not be separately included in the financial statements. The principle of materiality will decide which to show separately. An item is material and should be disclosed separately in the accounts if its misstatement or omission might reasonably be expected to influence the users of those accounts. Conversely, if too much detail is included, the understand ability of the information given in the accounts can be impaired. It is therefore a judgement call by the trustees.

While smaller PCCs (those below the audit threshold) do not have to follow these activity headings, it is strongly recommended that they do so. This will make it easier for those who wish to compare PCC accounts and for the completion of annual Returns of Parish Finance (RPF) to the diocese or Archbishops' Council. The relevant RPF note number has been included alongside each account description.

The headings in the Category column correspond to the SORP 2005 requirements and should be disclosed on the face of the Statement of Financial Activities as needed. Only where the amount is material should an individual Account Heading be disclosed on either the face of the SOFA or in the notes. Nor should they be disclosed even in the notes to the financial statements, unless they are considered material enough to do so.

Further detail on each of the items in the Account Description column can be found in the Receipts and Payments Guide and the Church of England Annual Return of Parish Finance Receipts and Payments Categories.

4.20 Categorisation of Incoming and expended resources

The following categories are recommended for use by all PCCs:

Incoming Resources

Category	Account Heading	Account Description	RPF Note
Voluntary Income	Planned giving	Gift Aid – Bank	01
		Gift Aid – Envelopes	01
		Other planned giving	02
	Collections at Services	Loose plate collections	03
		Special collections	03
	All other giving/ voluntary	Gift Days	04
		Giving through church boxes	04
		Donations appeals etc	05
		Gifts of freehold or leasehold land or of quoted shares/securities at market value	05
		Legacies (ensure accounting dealt with elsewhere)	07
		Recurring grants	08
		Non-recurring one-off grants	08A
		Donated services and facilities: The quantified 'value to the charity' of donated assistance that the PCC would otherwise have had to purchase to meet its actual needs. Include in the most appropriate category.	Include in the most appropriate category.
	Gift Aid recovered	Gift Aid recovered This must be shown separately and, if no tax recovery claim has been made, an explanation should be given in a note to the financial statements.	06
Activities for generating funds	Fund-raising	Church fetes, rummage sales, bazaars, etc.	09
		Book stall – non-church purposes	09
		Book stall – non-church purposes	09
		Church hall lettings – non objects related	09
		Parish magazine – advertising	12
Investment Income	Income from Investments	Dividends	10
		Bank and building society interest	10
		Rent from lands or buildings owned by the PCC	10
Church Activities	Income from church activities	Fees for weddings and funerals	11
		Fees for courses, groups and events	11
		Book stall and magazine sales – objects related	12
		Church hall lettings – objects related	12

Other incoming resources	Other incoming resources	Insurance claims – Where the insurer pays a supplier's bill direct that amount might or might not count as income. This depends on the nature of the insurance policy.	13
		Gain on sales of fixed assets held for the PCC's own use – sale proceeds less net book value	13
		Other incoming resources not covered elsewhere	13

Resources expanded

Category	Account Heading	Account Description	RPF Note
Church Activities	Parish Share/Quota / Family Purse	Parish Share/Quota /Family Purse	19
	Church Running Expenses	Salaries and wages of parish staff	20
		National Insurance of parish staff	20
		Pension Contributions of parish staff	20
		Working expenses of clergy	21
		Council tax	21
		Parsonage house expenses	21
		Water rates – vicarage	21
		Clergy telephone	21
		Visiting speakers / locums	21
		Education	21
		Parish training and mission	21/22
		Church running – insurance	22
		Church office – telephone	23
		Organ / piano tuning	23
		Church maintenance	23
		Cleaning	23
		Upkeep of services	23
		Upkeep of churchyard	23
		Printing, postage and stationery	23
		Church running – depreciation	24
		Church running – electric, oil and gas	24
		Church running – water	24
		Magazine & books expenses – PCC objects related	25
		Other Church Running Expenses	23
	Hall Running Costs (and other PCC functional properties)	Hall running – oil	25
		Hall running – electricity	25

		Hall running – gas	25
		Hall running – insurance	25
		Hall running – maintenance	25
		Hall running – telephone	25
		Hall running – water	25
		Hall running – depreciation	25
	Church Repairs & Maintenance	Church major repairs – structure	27
		Church major repairs – installation	27
		Church interior and exterior decorating	27
	Hall (& other PCC properties) Repairs & Maintenance	Hall + major repairs – structure	28
		Hall + major repairs – installation	28
		Hall + interior and exterior decorating	28
		Other PCC property upkeep	28
	Mission Giving and Donations	Giving to missionary societies	18
		Giving – relief and development agencies	18
		Other donations to support wider mission work outside the Parish.	18
Cost of generating funds	Costs of generating voluntary income	Fees paid to professional fund raisers	17
		Costs of applying for grants	17
		Costs of stewardship campaign	17
	Fundraising trading: cost of goods sold and other costs	Costs of fetes and other events	17
		Bookstall cost of goods for fund-raising purposes and associated running costs	17
	Investment management costs	Investment management costs	17
Governance Costs	Governance Costs	Independent Examination/Audit Costs	26
		Costs of trustee training/PCC meetings	26
Other resources expended	Other resources expended	Any resources expended that the PCC has not been able to analyse within the other resources expended categories. (Losses on fixed assets should be treated as additional depreciation under the appropriate heading).	Include in the most appropriate category.

4.21 Support costs

If support costs are separately identified and apportioned the basis for doing this should be reported in the note to the accounts (see Chapter 2, section 2.13).

chapter 5

The Balance Sheet

This chapter describes how assets and liabilities should be accounted for by PCCs. In some cases the rules set out in the Charities SORP and/or the current Financial Reporting Standard for Smaller Entities (the FRSSE which, being the 'most suitable' to its circumstances, should be adopted as the PCC's general accounting policy) cannot be applied by the PCC without modification.

5.1 Format

An example Balance Sheet is shown below. The Balance Sheet should be supported by notes. A full example, including notes summarising the movements in significant individual funds, is shown in Appendix ii.

The funds of a PCC should be grouped by kind, distinguishing between endowments, other restricted funds, designated and other unrestricted funds. The notes should distinguish any material individual funds among them and explain their nature and purpose.

In the notes to the balance sheet, the assets and liabilities representing those funds of the PCC should be clearly analysed between those funds. The notes should indicate whether or not sufficient resources are held in an appropriate form to enable each fund to be applied in accordance with the restrictions (if any) imposed on it. For example, if a PCC has a fund which is to be spent in the near future, it should be made clear in the notes whether or not the assets held in the fund are short-term assets.

In addition, the assets and liabilities should be analysed in a way that enables the reader to gain a proper appreciation of their spread and character. PCCs should not feel restricted by the formats provided in this chapter and are expected to provide more detail or analysis of the items concerned where this will lead to a better understanding of the financial statements. For example, long-term debtors (i.e. due only after more than one year) should, where the total is material, be separately stated in the balance sheet – otherwise their total amounts by category should be disclosed in the notes to the financial statements.

PAROCHIAL CHURCH COUNCIL OF ST LEDGER, AMBRIDGE

BALANCE SHEET AT 31 DECEMBER 2012

	Notes	2012 £	2011 £
FIXED ASSETS			
Tangible	6(a)	34,000	37,000
Investments	6(b)	13,625	14,500
		47,625	51,500
CURRENT ASSETS			
Stock		150	150
Investments	7(a)	24,060	15,000
Debtors and prepayments	7(b)	9,675	4,000
Short term deposits		11,000	8,000
Cash at bank and in hand		4,200	1,985
		49,085	29,135
LIABILITIES			
Creditors – amounts falling due within one year	8	2,700	4,450
NET CURRENT ASSETS / (LIABILITIES)		46,385	24,685
TOTAL ASSETS LESS CURRENT LIABILITIES		94,010	76,185
Creditors – amounts falling due after one year		500	1,000
TOTAL NET ASSETS		93,510	75,185
PARISH FUNDS			
Unrestricted	10	83,240	58,935
Restricted	10	7,775	14,000
Endowment	10	2,495	2,250
		93,510	75,185

Approved by the Parochial Church Council on 1 March 2013 and signed on its behalf by: The Revd James Colossae (PCC chairman), Mr David Jones (Vice Chairman and Church Warden)

5.2 Assets and their valuation

All assets of material value held for use on a continuing basis (i.e. two years or more) in the PCC's activities should be classified as fixed assets for PCC use and included in (or excluded from) the balance sheet. Most of these fixed assets are likely to be tangible assets, such as property or equipment, which are used in the course of the PCC's activities. Land and buildings held primarily for investment purposes should be classified as 'investment properties' and included with investments.

In order to account correctly for assets, PCCs need to understand what funds they hold in trust, what funds are held on their behalf for which they are responsible, and how they should value the assets of all these funds according to their use. In general terms, assets for which PCCs are responsible fall into the following groups for accounting purposes:

- Intangible assets

- Tangible fixed assets used for the work of the PCC:

  - Land & buildings

  - Motor vehicles

  - Fixtures, fittings and equipment

- Investment assets other than social (project-related) investments

- Social (project-related) investment assets

- Current assets

5.3 Intangible assets

An example of these is copyright royalties. These are very rare in practice and so no detail is included here.

5.4 Tangible fixed assets used for the work of the PCC

Tangible fixed assets include land and buildings, both freehold and leasehold, other than those held primarily for investment purposes and motor vehicles and fixtures, fittings and equipment.

The basic rule is found in paragraph 6.19 of the FRSSE: 'A tangible fixed asset shall initially be measured at its cost, then written down to its recoverable amount if necessary. The initial carrying amount of a tangible fixed asset received as a gift or donation by a charity shall be its current value, i.e. the lower of replacement cost and recoverable amount, at the date it is received. Where there is no record of the purchase price or production cost of an asset, or any such record cannot be obtained without unreasonable expense or delay, the value ascribed must be the earliest available record of its value. Particulars must be given of any case where the purchase price or production cost of any asset is for the first time determined in this way.'

Valuations may be obtained from a suitably qualified person, who could be a trustee or employee, for any class of fixed assets for which the PCC adopts a policy of accounting at 'current value' instead of at historical cost as above. There are no other alternatives to these two bases (see 5.12).

A number of PCCs have assets, e.g. historic buildings which are used by the church, for example for worship, but valuing them when they have not been previously included in accounts in order to follow the above rules might be impractical. This is because reliable historical cost/value information is not available and alternative valuation approaches (such as using the current cost of construction) lack sufficient reliability (e.g., in ignoring land-values) as a measure of 'current value'. In such cases they should not be valued in the accounts but the notes should contain a statement to that effect, explaining the reasons why. The notes should also contain information that enables the reader to appreciate the age, scale and nature of the excluded assets and the use made of them and their present condition.

5.5 Depreciation of fixed assets held for the PCC's own use

Most tangible fixed assets depreciate, that is wear out with the passing of time or become obsolete. Their value is thus expended over their useful economic life. This expenditure is recognised as depreciation in the Statement of Financial Activities and deducted from the assets' carrying value in the balance sheet.

Fixed assets held for functional (church) use which are included in the balance sheet and are considered to have a finite useful life should be depreciated at annual rates to spread their cost to the PCC evenly over their useful life in each case. An example of such assets is a computer used in the church office. In addition, if recently acquired movable church furnishings are included (because they have either been valued or recently acquired), they should also be depreciated. PCCs should set a threshold below which fixed assets are considered too small to include in the balance sheet ('capitalise'). Many PCCs set a threshold (of perhaps £500 or £1,000) below which fixed assets are included in expenditure rather than in the balance sheet.

This annual depreciation charge should be included in the appropriate cost category in the SOFA, and the accumulated depreciation will appear in the balance sheet as a deduction from the value of the relevant fixed assets.

To achieve the correct attribution of depreciation and to identify the nature of fixed assets held, fixed assets should be divided between those used primarily in direct furtherance of the PCC's objects (for example, church halls and PCC-owned houses) and those which are primarily retained and used to generate income (for example, a house available for rental on the open market).

If a house is retained primarily to generate rent rather than for the church's own use then it will be an investment property and will not be depreciated.

Where a fixed asset used for the functioning of the PCC and included at a value in the balance sheet has suffered permanent diminution in value or 'impairment' (this is unlikely to be a frequent occurrence), the loss should be recognised by means of an impairment charge in the SOFA.

In determining whether the balance sheet value of any individual asset has become 'impaired', changes in the value of other assets should not be taken into account.

The Church of England has complex rules about ownership of assets. PCCs may be trustees of income and expenditure relating to assets of which they are not the legal owner* and in relation to which they are not accountable under Part 8 of the Charities Act 2011. (*The FRSSE requires a 'substance over form' approach by defining 'assets' for inclusion in the accounts as 'rights or other access to future economic benefits controlled by an entity as a result of past transactions or events' – which clearly goes beyond legal ownership unless exclusion is statutory.) Most PCCs will be in the following position with regard to their tangible fixed assets:

5.6 Land and buildings

The parish have maintenance responsibility for the consecrated land/buildings and certain other (benefice) properties within the parish. The Charities Act 2011 states in Section 10(2) that benefice property (sub-section (a) and consecrated property (sub-section (c)) are removed from the definition of charity for the purposes of the Act. Therefore these assets should not be included in the financial statements though they may be referred to in the notes. Costs associated with the maintenance or improvement of such assets will be written off in the year they are incurred. This exclusion includes the parsonage house.

In law 'consecration' is not considered to be the same as 'dedication' as the latter is no more than an expression of pious intention that the building or land is given back to God. By act of consecration, property is effectively dedicated to God and set aside solely for sacred purposes.

Where a parish has other buildings, the legal title to these is likely to be held by a diocesan body on their behalf. As fixed assets of the PCC which are held for continuing use in its work, these should all be included in the Balance Sheet and shown under the appropriate fund heading to indicate which fund they belong to.

Land and buildings can be left at cost or re valued to 'current value'. If a revaluation policy is adopted it must be for all assets within that asset-class, with the carrying values updated on a regular basis, and the trustees may use any reasonable approach to valuation at least every five years, with reviews in between to consider if there have been any material changes.

Great care should be taken if using the insured value for balance sheet valuation purposes, unless the insurance is for only the fair value of the asset taking into account its existing condition (i.e. 'total loss' replacement cost less a deduction for wear and tear to date) and the current land value (for existing use) is added in. The value in a 'replacement as new' policy would need to be modified to bring it to a fair value.

Building and leasehold properties will need to be depreciated over their estimated useful lives in accordance with a disclosed policy. A policy of non-depreciation can only be adopted if both the annual depreciation charge and the accumulated depreciation are immaterial to the financial statements, due to the asset having a very long remaining useful life (i.e., 50 years or more), and/or the estimated residual value (discounted for price-inflation since the date of acquisition) is high.

If no depreciation is charged, on the basis of immateriality, then an impairment review may need to be undertaken annually. This need not be onerous as it seeks to establish some indication that the amount an asset is carried at on the balance sheet is less than both of the sale value, or the value of the use the asset provides to the parish.

Freehold land should not be depreciated.

The parish has responsibility for ensuring that the buildings are adequately insured and it is recommended, though not mandatory, that the insurance valuation of the buildings (including consecrated and benefice buildings) is included in a note to the financial statements for reference.

5.7   Motor vehicles and fixtures, fittings and equipment

The various items of movable church furnishings are vested in the churchwardens for the use and benefit of the parishioners and cannot be disposed of without a faculty. These assets are regarded as 'inalienable' property held on special trust on behalf of the PCC, and (unless forming part of the consecrated property excluded from accounts by the Charities Act) should be capitalised and disclosed in the fixtures, fittings and equipment asset category under the appropriate fund.

In addition to fixtures, fittings and equipment described above, the parish will have 'functional equipment' that is used on a continuing basis for the work of the PCC. Examples include: office equipment (computers etc.), ground and building maintenance equipment and vehicles. These are fixed assets and (apart from any immaterial items which have been treated as an expense) should be included in the Balance Sheet – this will normally be at cost less depreciation.

The notes to the financial statements should also summarise all changes in the amounts of each category of fixed assets as shown in the balance sheet and reconcile the opening and closing balances on each one. This means separate reconciliations of the cost to date (or the valuation, where the 'current value' option under the accounting standards (see 5.4) has been chosen since 2000) and of the depreciation or amortization provided. Similarly the notes should show the movements in investment fixed assets (see note 6 in Appendix ii).

5.8   Investment fixed assets

Investment fixed assets include properties held wholly or primarily for investment purposes, as well as investment securities and long term cash deposits. Investment fixed assets must be valued at their open market value (where practicable) unless made in furtherance of a charitable purpose, in which case as 'social investments' they should be carried at historical cost less any amounts now deemed irrecoverable. This would include 'soft loans' made for Church purposes.

5.9 Current assets

Current assets include stocks (of paper, cards etc.), debtors, investment assets currently held for disposal without reinvestment and cash at bank and in hand. They should be recognised at the lower of their cost and their net realisable value – other than investment assets (see paragraph 5.8).

Current assets should be subdivided by category, where applicable, to show:

(i)   stock (for example heating oil, bookstall publications);

(ii)   debtors, which should be further analysed in the notes between:

      (a)   debtors for goods and services (for example rents receivable on premises letting);

      (b)   amounts owed by an institution or body corporate which is a related party to the PCC;

      (c)   other debtors (for example amounts owed by HMRC);

      (d)   prepayments and accrued income.

(iii)   investment assets (only applicable where the PCC intends to spend the proceeds of sale on activities instead of reinvesting them); and

(iv)   cash at bank and in hand (including deposits with the CBF Church of England Funds or a Diocesan Board of Finance).

The notes applicable to showing the movement in investment assets held as fixed assets also apply to investment assets held as current assets – which the SORP also requires to be shown at their current market value, even if this exceeds their historical cost.

5.10 Current liabilities and long-term liabilities

Current liabilities include loans and overdrafts, trade creditors, amounts owed to subsidiary undertakings, other creditors and accrued expenses and deferred income. They should be recognised on the balance sheet at their settlement value. Amounts due after more than one year should be separately disclosed.

Liabilities should be analysed between those payable within a year (short-term) and others (long-term), with the total (if material) of any provisions for liabilities shown separately.

The totals for both short-term and long-term liabilities should be sub-analysed in the notes between:

(i)   loans and overdrafts;

(ii)   creditors for goods and services;

(iii)   amounts owed to any institution or body corporate which is a related party to the PCC;

(iv)   accrued expenses and deferred income (for example, an estimate of fuel unbilled up to the year-end); and

(v)   If a PCC has not fully paid its parish share but has indicated to the DBF that it intends to make further payment towards the outstanding amount, that payment should be included as a creditor in the balance sheet. If for whatever reason a PCC's full parish share is not to be met, this fact should be mentioned in the annual report to enable a full understanding of the PCC's financial affairs.

5.11 Heritage assets

Heritage assets are assets of historical or artistic importance that are held primarily to advance preservation, conservation and educational objectives of charities and in order through public access to contribute in themselves to the nation's culture and education at either national or local level. Such assets are central to the achievement of the purposes of such charities and include the land, buildings, structures, collections, exhibits or artefacts that are preserved or conserved and are central to the educational objectives of such charities. The primary objective of any PCC is not the preservation of the buildings they occupy or the furnishings and other artefacts for which they are responsible and none of a PCC's assets will therefore be heritage assets, even though some may be of considerable historical or artistic importance.

5.12 Accounting bases

The methods and principles on which assets are to be included in the Balance Sheet are illustrated in the model set of accounting policies in Chapter 2.

CATEGORY	CLASS	RECOGNITION	VALUATION
Intangible assets		Include if purchased	Historical cost (no revaluations allowed under the FRSSE)
Tangible fixed assets	Consecrated land and buildings and other property Parsonage house	Not included in accounts May note existence in TAR	No valuation required
	Freehold land & buildings (e.g. PCC-owned house, church hall)	Include	Cost or valuation in use, less depreciation (no depreciation on land)
	Leasehold land & buildings

Motor vehicles

Fixtures, fittings and equipment – including movable church furnishings (unless forming part of 'consecrated property') | Include | Cost or valuation in use, less depreciation |
| Investment fixed assets | Investment properties

Financial investments securities

Long-term cash deposits | Include | Market value |
| Social investments | Securities; 'soft' loans | Include | Historical cost less irrecoverable amounts |
| Current assets | Investments shortly to be disposed of for spending | Include | Market value |
| | Stock

Debtors

Cash at bank/in hand | Include | Lower of cost or realisable value |
| Liabilities and long-term creditors | Loans and overdrafts

Other creditors

Accruals and deferred income | Include | The value at which the liability will be settled |

chapter 6

The Annual Report

Introduction

The preparation of a written annual report, like the preparation of the financial statements, is the joint responsibility of the whole PCC. It puts all the PCC's financial statements into perspective and relates them to the wider life of the church. It will review the past year and link financial plans to the vision for the future. For this reason, while it is legally a separate document from the financial statements, the annual report and accounts (including the independent examiner/audit report) should always be presented together in the same publication.

The Church Representation Rules (Rule 9(1) (b)) require 'an annual report on the proceedings of the parochial church council and the activities of the parish generally' to be received by the Annual Parochial Church Meeting (APCM). The meeting is then free to discuss it.

The report is quite separate from the statement or address that the incumbent may wish to make to the APCM.

The Church Accounting Regulations 2006 no longer contain specific requirements as to the information to be included in the annual report, but simply refer to the need to comply with the Charities Act, any regulations made there under and SORP 2005. The detailed requirements are in paragraphs 6.1 to 6.10 below.

The report will usually be drafted by the secretary and the treasurer of the PCC, but some PCCs may wish to involve others in the drafting. It is a significant document in the life of the church and should be prepared in that light rather than as a chore to be completed.

The PCC must adopt the report before it is presented to the APCM and it must be dated and signed by the chairman of the PCC meeting at which it was adopted. Ideally an early draft should be shown to the PCC, but beware attempting to draft by committee.

The independent examiner or the auditor will need to see at least a draft of the report as a part of their scrutiny of the financial statements.

Because the report must be written for the general public as well as for church members, it has to include information that church members might take for granted, such as identification of the parish church, how the PCC operates and the names of its members.

The whole report should deal with the main activities of the church and new developments planned. It will give a flavour of the church at worship, 'being' as well as 'doing', through its pastoral ministry and mission outreach showing how it relates to those outside and on the fringes as well as in the congregation.

It is in no one's interest to make the report long and complicated. It is much more likely to be read if it is succinct and to the point. PCCs that have access to computers and desk top publishing facilities will want to make the layout attractive and may wish to include graphs, graphics and photographs.

The report should explain the governance and management structure and enable the reader to understand how the numerical part of the financial statements relates to the organisational structure and activities of the PCC. (See the example at the end of this chapter.)

The full content of the report is recommended as best practice for all PCCs, but for all those PCCs which are below the audit threshold there are significant reductions in the disclosures.

The following sections outline the requirements that all PCCs must report. There are however specific mandatory requirements for PCCs where their income is above the current audit threshold of £500,000. **These additional reporting requirements (which may still be included by those below the audit threshold) are shown in italics at the end of each section.**

6.1 Aim and purposes

This section establishes the framework under which the PCC has operated in the year and its intentions. It should provide a statement of the aims and objects of the PCC. The primary object of all PCCs will be the promotion of the Gospel of our Lord Jesus Christ according to the doctrines and practices of the Church of England. The Parochial Church Councils (Powers) Measure states the PCC 'is to cooperate with the minister in promoting in the parish the whole mission of the Church, pastoral, evangelistic, social and ecumenical'. Some parishes may have 'mission' or 'vision' statements they wish to include.

Although all charities have always had to meet the public benefit requirement, the Charities Act highlights it by requiring all charities to demonstrate, explicitly, that their aims are for the public benefit, including charities advancing education or religion, or relieving poverty, which were previously presumed to be for the public benefit.

Public benefit is assessed by two key principles:

1)   There must be an identifiable benefit or benefits.

2)   The benefit must be to the public, or section of the public.

The level of detail a PCC must provide will depend on whether their charity is above or below the audit threshold.

For those below the audit threshold, the PCC must include a brief summary in their Annual Report of the main activities undertaken explaining how these furthered the charity's aims for the public benefit. The summary should also confirm that the PCC has had regard to the Charity Commission public benefit guidance, where relevant. The PCC can, of course, provide fuller public benefit statements if they wish.

For those, above the audit threshold, the PCC must provide a fuller explanation in their Annual Report of the significant activities undertaken in order to carry out the PCC's aims for the public benefit, as well as their aims and strategies. They must explain their achievements, measured by reference to the PCC's aims and to the objectives. It is up to the PCC to decide how much detail they want to provide to clearly illustrate what their charity has done in the reporting year to meet the requirement. The Charity Commission guidance states that 'a charity that said nothing on public benefit in its Trustees' Annual Report, or produced only the briefest statement with no detail, would be in breach of the public benefit reporting requirement'.

Public benefit should be demonstrated in the Objectives and Activities and Achievements and Performance sections.

6.2 Objectives and activities

This section establishes how the PCC is trying to fulfil the aims of the church. All PCCs should provide a summary of the main objectives and activities of the church in the year. This should include:

●   an explanation of the PCC's main objectives for the year. These may, largely, remain constant from year to year, but may also include a particular focus for a year which may either have been determined by the PCC (such as particular work on the buildings), or be led by the deanery or the diocese (such as mission and growth initiatives).

●   an explanation of the strategies and activities that have been adopted to enable the PCC to achieve its objectives. This could provide details of the programmes the church does, such as regular worship services; house groups; women's, men's and youth groups; drop-in centres; outreach work; etc.

●   *the costs of programmes and activities can be shown in the accounts and thus provide a direct link to the report;*

●   *the policy for making grants or donations should be given (including how potential recipients are identified). It will be rare for a PCC to have social or programme related investment activities but where these exist the policies adopted for the selection and management of these activities should be given.*

- *an explanation of the contribution of volunteers where they play a significant role either in the charitable activities of the PCC or in generating funds. This might include an explanation of the activities undertaken and the contribution in terms of hours or staff equivalents and may also include an indicative value of this contribution. Similarly, where the PCC has received unquantifiable free facilities or services during the year, it should explain briefly the extent to which it relies on these continuing in order to pursue its work.*

6.3 Achievements and performance

This section details how the PCC should provide a summary of the main achievements of the church in the year. This could include:

- extracts from returns to the diocese on numbers of different types of services held and the attendance at the regular services, baptisms, confirmations, etc.

- details of the various special activities that the church ran during the year, e.g. missions, fund-raising for overseas mission, pilgrimages, community events, etc.

- a review of the charitable activities undertaken that explains the performance achieved against the objectives set. In some cases it will be possible to explain the outcomes in terms of numbers (such as numbers on the electoral roll and/or attendance figures). Much of the work of the church, however, cannot be reduced to numbers and in order to evaluate its achievements the PCC will need to draw on reports of experiences which may be oral or written.

- where the objectives set cover a longer term than the financial year, the review will take the form of a progress report;

- where they are material, a review of the performance of fund-raising activities against the objectives set for them;

- where material investments are held, details of investment performance against the investment objectives set;

- a commentary on those factors within and outside the PCC's control that are relevant to the achievement of the objectives. These might include relationships with employees, members of the congregation, and the church's position in the wider community. This is intended to give a context to the activities of the year: for example the departure of the incumbent or a key member of staff may, necessarily, curtail some of the work planned for the year.

6.4 Financial review

The report will paint a picture of the financial position of the church which will supplement the financial statements. They will assist the reader in understanding what it is that they are being asked to support financially and how those resources (and others) are being stewarded and used. It should also review the financial position of any subsidiary undertakings the church may have. This section of the report should also include:

- an explanation of the circumstances that have given rise to any fund which is materially in deficit and details of any steps being taken to eliminate that deficit;

- *details of the principal funding sources and how expenditure in the year under review has supported the key objectives of the PCC;*

- *where material investments are held, the investment policy and objectives, including the extent to which social, environmental or ethical considerations are taken into account.*

6.5　Reserves policy

The PCC should formulate and disclose its policy on reserves. The adoption of a policy on reserves will help to identify situations where a PCC may need to consider either reducing or increasing the level of reserves that it holds. For example, the church may be in receipt of income that more than covers all its running costs (including diocesan parish share). Money collected from parishioners is therefore over and above what the parish needs. Alternatively, there may be parishes where the reserves are too low to cope with the requirements of the PCC's cash flow.

In addition to stating the amount of reserves held, the report should explain what the PCC considers to be an appropriate level of free reserves, and what action the PCC proposes to take to reduce or increase its free reserves where necessary. This will show the parish that it is acting responsibly in holding the level of reserves that it holds. The public can then fully understand the availability and planned use of the PCC's funds. Even if the PCC has no free reserves, it should provide an explanation.

Free reserves are defined as that part of the PCC's income funds that is freely available. This definition of reserves therefore normally excludes:

(a)　permanent endowment funds;

(b)　expendable endowment funds;

(c)　restricted income funds;

(d)　any part of unrestricted funds which is not currently available for spending (e.g. income funds which can only be realised by disposing of fixed assets held for charity use).

Individual parishes may have more or less reserves than this simple calculation suggests. For example, they may have expendable endowments that can be spent (increasing reserves) or they may have designated some part of general funds for a particular project (reducing reserves). PCCs should report the amount of their reserves in the report.

6.6　Funds held as custodian trustees on behalf of others

In some circumstances the PCC may act as a custodian trustee for the assets of another charity. Where this is the case the report should give a brief description of the assets held; the name and objects of the charity on whose behalf they are held and an explanation of how this fits with the objects of the PCC; and details of the arrangements for the safe custody and segregation of such assets from those of the PCC.

6.7　Plans for future periods

The annual report should provide the reader with an explanation of the PCC's plans for the future (this will be the current year at the time the report is presented), including the key objectives and activities planned to support them. These will then form the basis of the objectives and activities section of the next report.

6.8　Risk management

While PCCs with a gross income of less than £500,000 are not required to state their risk management policy it is best practice for all PCCs to be aware of the risks and it is strongly recommended that all PCCs have a risk management policy.

PCCs are required to state in their annual report that the major risks to which the PCC is exposed have been reviewed and that systems or procedures designed to manage those risks have been established. This is the responsibility of the PCC.

For further details on Risk Management see the Charity Commission Guidance CC26 which is available on its website.

6.9 Structure, governance and management

This section should make clear to the reader the legal framework within which the PCC operates, and how decisions are made. It should include:

- An explanation of how the PCC is constituted. For most PCCs this will be as shown below. However, a PCC which is a team ministry or part of a united benefice should briefly outline how it is established here.

  'The Parochial Church Council is a corporate body established by the Church of England. The PCC operates under the Parochial Church Council Powers Measure. The PCC is a Registered Charity (or where the PCC has gross income under £100,000 and is not a registered charity – "The PCC is excepted by order from registering with the Charity Commission").'

- A statement that the appointment of PCC members is governed by and set out in the Church Representation Rules.

- *If the PCC has any related trusts or charities, an explanation of the relationship of the PCC to these trusts.*

- *The policies and procedures adopted for the recruitment, induction and training of PCC members. As the PCC has ultimate responsibility for a wide range of matters affecting the parish, including such matters as compliance with health and safety, disability discrimination legislation and child protection, it is important that the PCC adopts appropriate training procedures. These are likely to include training courses arranged by the diocese or deanery which are attended by a PCC representative who reports back to the PCC as a body, and the dissemination of reading matter.*

- *A brief description of the way the PCC organises itself in order to carry out its aims and objectives. Many PCCs will probably have only a Standing Committee, but others may well have various committees. The purpose or terms of reference of the committees should be summarised. This should make clear the types of decision which are delegated to committees or to the incumbent or administrator.*

- *A statement confirming that the major risks to which the PCC is exposed, as identified by the PCC members, have been reviewed and systems or procedures have been established to manage those risks.*

6.10 Administrative information

This information should be given each year; even though much of it may be the same as for the previous year, it may be recorded separately from the main body of the report:

- the full name (town/village and church dedication) of the PCC;

- the location of the church (or address if it has one) and the PCC correspondence address. This could be the church office (if there is one), that of the incumbent or of an officer of the PCC that can be made public;

- the charity registration number (where applicable);

- the names of all the members of the PCC who have served since the commencement of the financial year until the approval of the financial statements. The names of those who have left the PCC and the names of those who have replaced them should be given. This is a list of all those who have been trustees of the charity. Those who have been officers of the PCC should be indicated;

- *the names and addresses of bankers, legal and other advisers to the PCC, and of the independent examiner or auditor;*

- *the name of the person or persons to whom day-to-day management is delegated, e.g. the incumbent.*

Example Trustees' Annual Report (TAR)

2012 Report and Accounts for the Parochial Church Council of St Ledger's Church, Ambridge

Aim and purposes

St Ledger's Parochial Church Council (PCC) has the responsibility of cooperating with the incumbent, the Reverend James Colossae, in promoting in the ecclesiastical parish, the whole mission of the Church, pastoral, evangelistic, social and ecumenical. The PCC is also specifically responsible for the maintenance of the Church Centre complex of St Ledger's, The Green, Ambridge.

Objectives and activities

The PCC is committed to enabling as many people as possible to worship at our church and to become part of our parish community at St Ledger. The PCC maintains an overview of worship throughout the parish and makes suggestions on how our services can involve the many groups that live within our parish. Our services and worship put faith into practice through prayer and scripture, music and sacrament.

When planning our activities for the year, we have considered the Commission's guidance on public benefit and, in particular, the supplementary guidance on charities for the advancement of religion. In particular, we try to enable ordinary people to live out their faith as part of our parish community through:

- Worship and prayer; learning about the gospel; and developing their knowledge and trust in Jesus.
- Provision of pastoral care for people living in the parish.
- Missionary and outreach work.

To facilitate this work it is important that we maintain the fabric of the Church of St Ledger and the Church Centre Complex.

Achievements and performance

Worship and prayer

The PCC is keen to offer a range of services during the week and over the course of the year that our community find both beneficial and spiritually fulfilling. For example, evening prayers provide a quiet, intimate and reflective environment for worship while opportunities are provided for people to engage in more outgoing worship such as that provided by the youth group within our parish.

This year we have been successful in welcoming more families into our church and have agreed a new style of Family Worship on the morning of the 3rd Sunday each month. This has meant that special arrangements have had to be made for baptisms and for welcoming the families at corporate worship on the 1st Sunday of each month. It is pleasing to be able to report that the new arrangements have been well received since they came into operation during September. They will be reviewed by the PCC after 12 months. In addition, a great deal of time and thought was spent during the year on making best use of the new services. Many have said how much easier it is to follow the services now that they are printed out in booklets.

All are welcome to attend our regular services. At present there are 173 parishioners on the Church Electoral Roll, 91 of whom are not resident within the parish. 18 names were added during the year and 9 were removed either through death or because they moved away from the parish. The average weekly attendance, counted during October, was 107, but this number increased at festivals and two Christmas carol services had to be held to seat all those who wished to attend.

As well as our regular services, we enable our community to celebrate and thank God at the milestones of the journey through life. Through baptism we thank God for the gift of life, in marriage public vows are exchanged with God's blessing and through funeral services friends and family express their grief and give thanks for the life which is now complete in this world and to commend the person into God's keeping. We have celebrated 25 baptisms and 15 weddings and held 26 funerals in our church this year.

Deanery Synod

Three members of the PCC sit on the deanery synod. This provides the PCC with an important link between the parish and the wider structures of the church. This year the PCC has also focused its attention on the questions posed to parishes in the deanery about the most effective deployment of stipendiary and non-stipendiary clergy.

The Church Centre Complex

We want our church to be open to our community for private prayer. Unfortunately, since the theft of valuable church artefacts from St Augustus Church, in the neighbouring parish, we have felt unable to leave the church open at all times for private worship. We are however pleased that a rota of parishioners has enabled us to open the church at weekends and for all public holidays in the past year.

The state of the nave roof had been identified as a major concern for some time and despite routine maintenance being carried out, a detailed report on its condition prepared by the architect in April 2011 confirmed the need for major structural renewal and re-ordering. The work started in January 2012 and the total cost of the project was £189,000. Grants totalling £162,000 were received and a further £8,000 was raised from fund-raising. The PCC had decided not to start an appeal and would instead fund the shortfall of £19,000 from general funds (£10,000 had been designated in the previous year).

The kitchen in the Church Hall was refurbished during August and the new environment meets the stringent health and safety requirements and allows us to continue the old people's luncheon club on Saturdays. 18 people regularly attend at our luncheon club, 12 of whom are parishioners. We were particularly pleased to be able to extend the services of our club to the members of the Ambridge Green Methodist Chapel luncheon club when the death of Alice Luther, the main organiser of that club forced its closure.

During the week the hall is used by our mothers and toddlers group on Wednesdays. Fifteen children and their carers have been regular attenders at the mothers and toddlers group. During the summer the group organised two outings including older siblings during the school holidays. In July, twenty children and their parents went for the day to Longleat and later in the holidays we had the hottest day of the year for our family outing to New Milton.

The crèche runs in the hall on Tuesday and Thursday mornings. There are 12 regular attenders at the crèche which is organised by Sally Pincent, the council's peripatetic childcare coordinator who runs crèches at our church as well as at St Augustus on Mondays and Wednesdays. She has a rota of volunteers from the parish who help her all of whom have been CRB checked. The crèche had an OFSTED inspection during the year and passed with flying colours.

Pastoral care

Some members of our parish are unable to attend church due to sickness or age. Reverend James Colossae has visited all church members who have requested it, to celebrate communion with them either at their homes or in hospital. Miss Finching has continued to organise a rota of volunteers to visit all who are sick or unable to get out for any other reason to keep them in touch with church life.

Mission and evangelism

Helping those in need is a demonstration of our faith. The Mission and Evangelism Committee are to be congratulated on its fund-raising efforts. Missionary and charitable giving totaled £56,200. Three members of our congregation are working with the Moses Cain and Grace Cross charity which works with deprived children in the Far East. Thanks to the generosity of the congregation and the tireless work of John Leighton in securing grants, we were able to send £38,650 to support their work. £11,200 has been raised during the year to continue the support to CMS and £3,500 for the Ambridge Pensioners Club. Additionally this year £2,850 was raised for the Southern Africa Famine appeal.

Our parish magazine is distributed quarterly to all parishioners on the Church Electoral Roll and available at the Church Hall. The magazine keeps our parishioners informed of the important matters affecting our Church and articles that help develop our knowledge and trust in Jesus.

Ecumenical relationships

The church is a member of Churches Together in Ambridge and of the Wessex Interfaith Forum. We have held joint services on the fourth Sunday of every month with the Ambridge Green Methodist Church and for the first time this year have joined with them both for our Lent courses and to run an Alpha course in the autumn. The Alpha course has led a number of people to attend other church activities and services. We have also worked with Ambridge Green Methodist Church and Millfield Baptist Church to deliver a flyer to every home in the town advertising the Christmas services of all three churches.

Financial review

Total receipts on unrestricted funds were £193,650 of which £107,900 was unrestricted planned voluntary donations, and a further £24,050 was from Gift Aid. Restricted grants and donations of £216,750 were also received, the majority of which was for the major structural renewal project, and details are shown in the Financial Statements. The freehold house at 36 Church Road continues to be let temporarily, which provided a gross income of £4,200.

The planned giving through envelopes and banker's orders increased by 9% and it was good to see the use of Gift Aid envelopes increased. Total income, excluding legacies and exceptional income for the major structural renewal project and the Moses Cain and Grace Cross, went up by a healthy 13% compared with last year. This was mainly due to our stewardship campaign, whose theme was to give in grace, our time, talents and giving to reflect our deepening faith. We were grateful for a pecuniary legacy of £11,000 from the estate of Mrs Mary Rudge. £2,000 was set aside towards the cost of the much-needed cleaning of the organ. The work was completed in time for Christmas.

£154,300 was spent from unrestricted funds to provide the Christian ministry from St Ledger's Church, including the contribution to the diocesan parish share that increased by 5% in the year and largely provides the stipends and housing for the clergy.

The sum that the churches in the deanery have to find is shared between the churches according to a formula that is based mainly on a head count of the congregations. We have to find more of the sum at St Ledger's as the size of our congregation increased more compared with other churches.

Net movement in funds on unrestricted funds was £24,305 including £5,455 net gain on revaluation of investment assets. There was a small overspend on the restricted funds of £6,225. During the year, the total fund balances increased from £75,185 to £93,510 of which £83,240 is unrestricted.

Reserves policy

It is PCC policy to try to maintain a balance on free reserves (net current assets) which equates to at least three months' unrestricted payments. This is equivalent to £39,000. It is held to smooth out fluctuations in cash flow and to meet emergencies. The balance of the free reserves at the year end was £45,885 which is marginally higher than this target.

The balance of £7,775 in the restricted fund is retained towards meeting the upkeep of the Church Hall.

It is our policy to invest the short-term investment fund balances with the CCLA Church of England Deposit Fund, and the remainder in the CCLA Church of England Investment Fund.

Volunteers

We would like to thank all the volunteers who work so hard to make our church the lively and vibrant community it is. In particular we want to mention our churchwardens Mrs Cartwright and Mr Jones who have worked so tirelessly on our behalf and Mrs Nunn who has helped us all to understand the church's accounts and its finances.

Structure, governance and management

The Parochial Church Council is a corporate body established by the Church of England. The PCC operates under the Parochial Church Council Powers Measure. The PCC is a Registered Charity.

The method of appointment of PCC members is set out in the Church Representation Rules. At St Ledger's the membership of the PCC consists of the incumbent (our vicar), churchwardens, the reader and members elected by those members of the congregation who are on the electoral roll of the church. All those who attend our services / members of the congregation are encouraged to register on the Electoral Roll and stand for election to the PCC.

The PCC members are responsible for making decisions on all matters of general concern and importance to the parish including deciding on how the funds of the PCC are to be spent. New members receive initial training into the workings of the PCC.

The full PCC met six times during the year with an average level of attendance of 80%. Given its wide responsibilities the PCC has a number of committees each dealing with a particular aspect of parish life. These committees, which include worship, mission and outreach and fabric and finance, are all responsible to the PCC and report back to it regularly with minutes of their decisions being received by the full PCC and discussed as necessary.

Administrative information

St Ledger's Church is situated in The Green, Ambridge. It is part of the Diocese of Wessex within the Church of England. The correspondence address is The Vicarage, Church Street, Ambridge. Registered charity number 123456.

PCC members who have served at any time from 1 January 2012 until the date this report was approved are:

Ex Officio members:

Incumbent:	The Reverend James Colossae (Chairman)
Reader:	Mr Geoffrey Amis
Wardens:	Mrs Jean Cartwright
	Mr David Jones (Vice chairman)

Elected members:

Mr Alex Tipshaw, representative on Deanery Synod

Mr Peter Ackworth (Secretary), representative on Deanery Synod

Mr Jack Pierce, representative on Deanery Synod

Miss Fiona Fielding (From 5 April 2012)

Mrs Chloe Nunn (Treasurer)

Mr Gary Gledhill

Miss Henrietta Gordon

Mrs Tina Foster

Miss Hermione Ward (Until 5 April 2012)

Mr Martin Ward

Miss Emily Airedale

Mr Julian Footbridge (Until 5 April 2012)

Miss Lizzie Wrexham

Mr Ronald Nicholas (From 5 April 2012)

Approved by the PCC on 1 March 2013 and signed on their behalf by the Reverend James Colossae (PCC Chairman)

chapter 7

Group Consolidated Accounts and Annual Reports

This new statutory requirement was introduced in the 2006 Act for all (non-exempt) charities in control of subsidiary undertakings which, if charities themselves, do not count as a special trust or other 'charity branch' for inclusion in the entity accounts of the reporting charity. It applies only to those few PCCs whose combined gross income including all such subsidiaries exceeds the Charities Act current audit threshold of £500,000 for the year. The new requirement took effect for financial years commencing after March 2008, with the PCCs affected having to prepare group consolidated accounts for 2009 onwards.

Thus a PCC having trustee-body control of a connected charity from which it can draw benefit for its mission in the parish, but which it does not have to account for in its own accounts as a PCC, or (more rarely) beneficial control of a non-charitable body such as a wholly or partly owned trading company which it uses to generate additional revenues for the work of the PCC, will have to consolidate the statutory accounts of all such 'subsidiary undertakings' in group accounts to be prepared under s.138 of the Charities Act 2011, in addition to its own accounts, except to the extent that exemption can be claimed under s.139 of the Act.

For those group accounts, the SORP's recommendations are collected together in a special section as paragraphs 381–406 to show how charities can best comply with FRS2.

It should be noted here that PCCs adopting the FRSSE as their accounting policy (and only those few that cannot qualify as 'small' within the meaning of company law and the commercial financial reporting standards cannot do so) would have to extend their accounting policies disclosure if preparing group consolidated accounts. This is normally done by adding 'and other applicable financial reporting standards for the preparation of the consolidated accounts'. This is because the FRSSE says:-

> '2   Reporting entities that apply the FRSSE are exempt from complying with other accounting standards (Statements of Standard Accounting Practice and Financial Reporting Standards) and Urgent Issues Task Force (UITF) Abstracts, unless preparing consolidated financial statements, in which case certain other accounting standards apply …' and

> '16.2   Where the reporting entity is preparing consolidated financial statements, it should regard as standard the accounting practices and disclosure requirements set out in FRSs 2, 6, 7 and, as they apply in respect of consolidated financial statements, FRSs 5, 9, 10*, 11 and 28.'

SORP paragraphs 407-418, which deal with compliance with FRS9, also applies to any PCC not exempted from preparing consolidated accounts. FRS9 requires it to include in its accounts any material interests it may have in any kind (charitable or fund-raising) of consortium undertaking (corporate 'joint venture') or 'associated' undertaking (equity/voting interests above 20% but below the 50% of a joint venture, except where there is no significant influence on the investee's management) – as well as for what the SORP calls a 'joint arrangement'. The latter could obviously include any kind of participation in a non-corporate shared activity of a multi-denominational nature, thus not only the commercial kind of profit-sharing partnership activity that many companies engage in.

Parent charities invariably combine their group accounts with their entity accounts in the same publication, as this minimises the paperwork entailed and also allows them to take advantage of the SORP's non-statutory concession at paragraph 397 to publish their group SOFA without their own (entity) SOFA and instead to report the key figures from the latter as an accounts note.

The Group Accounts must be accompanied by a Group Annual Report, which replaces the usual PCC Annual Report. This Group Report includes specified disclosures in respect of the activities and performance of the subsidiary undertakings in relation to the PCC, but is otherwise the same as the Annual Report to be prepared by any other auditable PCC.

See Appendix iii for the group-accounting legislation contained in the 2011 Act and SI 2008/629.

chapter 8

Independent Examination

8.1 Introduction

The flowchart in Chapter 1, paragraph 1.2 sets out the thresholds for the independent examination and audit of PCC annual financial statements.

All PCCs below the audit threshold may choose to have their financial statements independently examined rather than audited. A major donor or grant maker may require the financial statements to be audited even though an independent examination might otherwise have been chosen. An audit is a more onerous form of scrutiny and must be carried out by a registered auditor but an auditor can be asked to act as an examiner. PCCs that can choose independent examination, rather than an audit, are encouraged to do so.

8.2 What does the PCC have to do?

A suitable examiner has to be appointed by the Annual Parochial Church Meeting (APCM). The PCC will have to consider carefully the suitability of a prospective independent examiner in good time in order to guide the meeting in its appointment.

8.3 Can an examiner be paid?

The PCC is entitled to pay a reasonable fee to an independent examiner for their services. If the services of a competent examiner cannot be obtained on a voluntary basis, the PCC should be prepared to pay a modest fee, which is a proper charge on its funds. The PCC should not be pressured into appointing an examiner acting in a voluntary capacity just because they will do the work free of charge. The PCC must be satisfied that the examiner has the requisite ability and experience.

8.4 Who can be an independent examiner?

An independent examiner is described in Section 145 of the Charities Act 2011 as

> 'an independent person who is reasonably believed by the trustees to have the requisite ability and practical experience to carry out a competent examination of the financial statements'

The term 'independent examiner' does not exclude an accountant or, indeed, a registered auditor, but recognises that the scrutiny is less onerous than an audit.

8.5 What does 'independent' mean?

● For an examiner to be independent that individual must have no connection with the PCC which might appear to be prejudicial to an impartial examination of the financial statements.

● The following persons will be considered to have a connection with the PCC that makes it inappropriate for them to be an examiner:

    (a) a member of the PCC or any of its sub-committees (this exclusion is included in the Church Representation Rules);

    (b) an employee of the PCC, or a person receiving benefit or support from PCC funds by way of a gift (other than a fee received as an examiner);

(c)   a child, parent, grandchild, grandparent, brother or sister, spouse, civil partner, business partner or employee of any person who falls within sub-paragraph (a) or (b) above.

● An independent examiner can, however, be a member of the Church with their name on the electoral roll.

8.6   What sort of people can be appointed?

● The Church Accounting Regulations require an external scrutiny of the financial statements for all PCCs, even though the Charities Act does not require external scrutiny where gross income is up to and including £25,000. It may be appropriate, for example, to appoint someone with basic bookkeeping skills as its independent examiner, if the financial statements are prepared on the receipts and payments basis.

● For PCCs with gross income that does not exceed £250,000 for the year, and with financial statements prepared on the receipts and payments basis, an appropriate independent examiner would be someone more familiar with business and financial matters. For all accruals accounts the examiner needs accountancy knowledge but they need not be a qualified accountant.

● PCCs with gross income between £250,000 and £500,000 for the year and with a balance sheet value of gross assets not exceeding £3.26 million, must appoint an appropriately qualified accountant or examiner (see CC32 on the Charity Commission website: www.charitycommission.gov.uk) to carry out the independent examination.

● PCCs with gross income in excess of £500,000 for the year, or where gross income is greater than £250,000 for the year and the balance sheet value of gross assets is in excess of £3.26 million, must have an audit by a registered auditor.

● Where group accounts, consolidating the accounts of the PCC and its subsidiaries, have to be prepared, the examiner must also have the requisite knowledge of the statutory group accounting requirements.

8.7   How should an examiner's requisite ability be checked?

Whether an examiner has the requisite ability will depend very much on the size and complexity of the PCC's financial statements as well as on the examiner's individual experience.

● The duty to seek evidence of the ability of a prospective independent examiner rests with the PCC. If the prospective independent examiner is not known to the members of the PCC, the PCC should consider asking to see a CV, taking independent references and possibly forming a small group to interview candidates.

● Difficulties can arise where the examiner has been recommended by an individual member of the PCC, who has then made the only contact with them. There have been cases where it was found that the examiner never existed!

8.8   What is appropriate 'practical experience'?

The PCC should satisfy itself that a prospective examiner has practical experience of preparing or reviewing and evaluating the financial statements of comparable organisations and can readily understand the PCC's financial statements.

8.9   How does the PCC know what it has to provide to the examiner?

The treasurer should discuss fully with the prospective examiner the work of the PCC and its expectations. Help will be found in these guidance notes on the duties of an examiner. In some dioceses guidance and advice may be available, or treasurers in neighbouring parishes or deanery finance officers may be in a position to assist. The examiner's duties must be followed to ensure that the requirements of the Church Accounting Regulations 2006 are met. The Charity Commission has produced guidance on independent examination in the following publications:

Independent Examination of Charity Accounts: Trustees' Guide (CC31)

Independent Examination of Charity Accounts: Examiners' Guide (CC32).

8.10 What happens when the PCC and the APCM appoint an examiner?

- Particularly for larger PCCs, it is recommended that, in order to reduce the chance of any misunderstanding, the independent examiner should write to the PCC detailing its accounting responsibilities and the examiner's statutory responsibilities. The content of the letter should be agreed with the PCC and a sample letter is shown below. The same distinction of responsibilities will normally be required by a professional examiner or auditor to be included in the annual report and accounts.

- Only examiners of PCCs with high income levels will probably document the agreed terms of engagement in this way, but the matters set out here should be discussed and agreed with all independent examiners prior to the examination.

- The examiner must be given sufficient time in which to complete the examination.

- The PCC will need to approve a motion for the appointment of the independent examination at the APCM. A suitable form of words is:

  The PCC has elected to subject the financial statements to independent examination and, therefore, having made appropriate enquiries, propose [insert the name of the examiner] as independent examiner until the next APCM.

Example: Letter setting out agreed Terms of Engagement for the independent examiner

[Note: The phrases in square brackets should be omitted when the examination is of accounts on the receipts and payments basis.]

The Secretary of the Parochial Church Council
St Ledger's Church

Dear members of the PCC,

Engagement as independent examiner

The purpose of this letter is to set out in confirmation of our recent discussions the basis on which I am prepared to act as independent examiner to prepare a report in respect of the PCC's financial statements for the year ended 31 December 2012, and for future years until further notice, in accordance with section 145 of the Charities Act 2011 ('the Act') and the Church Accounting Regulations 2006 ('the Regulations').

Responsibilities of members of the PCC

As members of the PCC, you are responsible for maintaining proper accounting records and for preparing accounts which [give a true and fair view and] have been prepared in accordance with the Regulations.

You are also responsible for determining whether, in respect of the year (and the preceding two years), the PCC meets the conditions for exemption from an audit of the accounts set out in section 144(1) of the Act and the Regulations, and for providing me with information and explanations required for my examination.

Responsibilities of the independent examiner

I shall plan my work on the basis that an independent examiner's report on the accounts is required for the year, unless you inform me in writing to the contrary. As an independent examiner I have a statutory duty to state in my report whether any matter has come to my attention in connection with the examination which gives me reasonable cause to believe that in any material respect:

a) accounting records have not been properly kept in accordance with section 130 of the Act; or

b) the accounts do not accord with the accounting records or do not comply with the Regulations [other than in respect of the requirement for a true and fair view].

I also have a statutory duty to disclose in my report [inconsistencies between the accounts and the annual report and] matters coming to my attention in connection with the examination to which, in my opinion, attention should be drawn in order to enable a proper understanding of the accounts to be reached.

Should my work lead me to conclude that the PCC is not entitled to exemption from an audit of the accounts or should I be unable to reach a conclusion on this matter, then I will not issue any report and will notify you in writing of the reasons. In these circumstances, if appropriate, I will discuss with you the need to appoint an auditor.

Scope of the independent examiner's work

My work will be carried out in accordance with general directions setting out the duties of an independent examiner issued by the Charity Commission and as contained in the Church guidance.

My work as independent examiner will be a less onerous form of scrutiny than an audit of the accounts in accordance with Auditing Standards. My examination will include a review of the accounting records kept by the PCC and a comparison of the accounts presented with those records. It will also include a review of the accounts and consideration of any unusual items or disclosures identified. In such cases where I identify an unusual item, I will seek explanations from the PCC, and may carry out verification and vouching procedures where I require further clarification. [Similarly I will make assessments of the estimates and judgements made by you in your preparation of the accounts where they are material to the accounts.]

My work cannot be relied on to identify the occasional omission or insignificant error, nor to disclose breaches of trust or statute, neglect or fraud which may have taken place and which it is the responsibility of the PCC to guard against.

Should I become aware, for any reason, that the accounts may be misleading and we cannot agree appropriate amendments, and I then conclude that the matter cannot be adequately dealt with in my report, I will not issue any report and will withdraw from the engagement, and will notify you in writing of the reasons.

As part of my normal procedures, I may request you to provide written confirmation of any information or explanations given by you orally during the course of my work.

Fees

I am prepared to waive my fee for this examination.

Confirmation

Once it has been agreed, this letter will remain effective until it is replaced or until I cease to hold the position of independent examiner. I shall be grateful if you will kindly confirm your agreement to the terms of this letter by arranging for the signature, and return, of the attached copy, or let me know if the terms of this letter are not in accordance with your understanding of my terms of appointment.

Yours faithfully

8.11 The Charity Commission's statutory Directions

- The Charity Commission's Directions provide the procedural basis or framework to define how the reporting duties of the examiner must be met. The Directions are made by the Charity Commission under powers given in the Charities Act 2011 and set out the areas of work that must be covered in any examination.

- The Charity Commission is aware that volunteer examiners, who are not charging a fee, are giving their time freely for the benefit of the charity sector. In the event of a concern arising about the adequacy of an independent examination carried out by a volunteer, the Commission will take into account the nature of the voluntary role and be proportionate in their approach when considering any failure in the examination process, provided the examiner has acted honestly and the PCC has acted diligently.

- Where the examiner is charging a fee or receiving payment it is expected that the services provided will be to a professional standard.

- In all cases the examiner:
    - must demonstrate appropriate technical knowledge, including familiarity with the Statement of Recommended Practice for Charities (the SORP) where accrual accounts are prepared;
    - must carry out their work fully in accordance with the Charity Commission's Directions; and
    - must be well placed, by virtue of their ability and experience, to fulfil their statutory duty to report matters of material significance to the Charity Commission.

- The actual Directions are contained in the Charity Commission's publication *Independent Examination of Charity Accounts: Examiners' Guide*.

  There are 10 Directions that the examiner must address in carrying out an examination of accrual accounts and 7 Directions applying to the examination of receipts and payments accounts. There is also a requirement for examiners to consider if matters of material significance have come to their attention which give rise to a legal duty to report to the Charity Commission. In terms of PCC accounts, these directions are summarised as follows:

Direction	Applicable to receipts and payments	Applicable to receipts and payments	Applicable to accruals and payments
1.	Examination and accounting thresholds	√	√
2.	Documentation	√	√
3.	Understanding the PCC	√	√
4.	Accounting records	√	√
5.	Comparison with accounting records	√	√
6.	Analytical procedures	√	√
7.	Form and content of financial statements		√
8.	Accounting policies, estimates and judgements		√
9.	The PCC's Annual Report	*	√
10.	Examiner's report	√	√
Statutory duty to report certain matters of material significance to the Charity Commission		√	√

*Although not mandatory, it is advisable for the examiner to read the Trustees' Report so that any special comments that the examiner needs to make in his/her report for a proper understanding of the accounts can be worded accordingly and not seemingly in isolation.

Further information regarding the Charity Commission's Directions is given in the following paragraphs. The Direction is in the box and the Charity Commission's guidance adapted for PCCs is below each box. The Directions are reproduced here to enable the PCC to understand clearly what the examiner will be asking for.

Direction 1 – Examination and accounting thresholds

> The examiner shall carry out such specific procedures as are considered necessary to provide a reasonable basis on which to conclude:

(i) that an examination is required under section 145(1) of the Charities Act 2011, and that section 144 (1) (audit) of the Charities Act 2011 does not apply to the charity; and

(ii) where accounts are prepared on a receipts and payments basis under section 133 of the Charities Act 2011, that the charity trustees may properly elect to prepare accounts under this sub-section.

- The PCC may elect for independent examination rather than full audit (under section 145 (1) of the Charities Act 2011), and may also elect for the preparation of receipts and payments accounts (under section 133) rather than the preparation of accruals accounts. For either election to be valid, the PCC must be within the relevant income threshold specified in the regulations for that election. The current thresholds are set out in the flowchart in paragraph 1.2.

- The examiner should therefore ascertain:

  - the PCC's gross income (see Chapter 1 for the definition of gross income) for the financial year concerned;

  - whether all subsidiary funds have been included in the calculations; and

  - whether any grant condition demands an audit of the statutory accounts.

- Carrying out these procedures at an early stage, particularly if the PCC is likely to pass the income threshold of £500,000 per annum, should prevent the work of the examiner being duplicated by a subsequent statutory audit which would add to the expenses for the PCC.

Direction 2 – Documentation

> The examiner shall record the examination procedures carried out and any matters which are important to support conclusions reached or statements provided in the examiner's report.

The independent examiner's working papers should provide details of the work undertaken and support any conclusions reached, and record any matters of judgement (where accruals accounts are prepared see Direction 8) which may arise. Working papers should normally be retained by the examiner for six years from the end of the financial year to which they relate, and would normally include:

- a letter of engagement from the independent examiner to the PCC;

- relevant information extracted or obtained from any governing document, PCC and other committee meeting minutes and a record of discussions with the PCC or its representatives;

- details of procedures carried out during the examination, with conclusions reached and any areas of concern identified;

- notes as to how any areas of concern have been resolved together with details of any verification procedures used;

- schedules showing the breakdown of accounting items that have been aggregated for accounts disclosure purposes;

- copies of any trial balance, financial statements and the PCC's annual report.

Direction 3 – Understanding the PCC

> The examiner shall obtain an understanding of the charity's constitution, organisation, accounting systems, activities and nature of its assets, liabilities, incoming resources and application of resources in order to plan the specific examination procedures appropriate to the circumstances of the charity.

For a proper examination to be carried out it is important for the examiner to have an understanding of the operations, structure and objectives of the PCC, as laid down in accordance with the Parochial Church Councils (Powers) Measure and the Church Representation Rules. This understanding will help the examiner to plan appropriate examination procedures. The steps taken by an examiner would normally include:

- consideration of the PCC's objects, powers and obligations, which are set out in the the the Parochial Church Councils (Powers) Measure;

- discussions with the PCC or its representatives to ascertain the structure, methods and means by which the PCC seeks to achieve its objects;

- discussions with the PCC or its representatives about the affairs and activities of the PCC in order to gain an insight into any special circumstances and problems affecting the PCC;

- reviewing the minutes of PCC and relevant committee meetings to ascertain details of major events, plans, decisions and any changes in the PCC's officers; and

- obtaining details of accounting records maintained, methods of recording financial transactions and financial control arrangements.

Direction 4 – Accounting records

> The examiner shall review the accounting records maintained in accordance with section 130 of the Charities Act 2011 in order to provide a reasonable basis for the identification of any material failure to maintain such records.

- The PCC is responsible for maintaining proper accounting records.

- The examiner is required to review the accounting records with a view to identifying any material failure to maintain such records in accordance with section 130 of the Charities Act 2011, which requires that they are sufficient to show and explain all the PCC's transactions, are capable of disclosing at any time the financial position of the charity with reasonable accuracy, and enable the PCC to ensure that any financial statements prepared by it comply with the form and content requirements set out in the Charities (Accounts and Reports) Regulations 2008.

- The review procedures are not aimed at identifying the occasional omission or insignificant error but at identifying any significant failure to maintain records in a manner consistent with statutory requirements.

- Accounting records should be well organised and capable of ready retrieval and analysis. The records may take a number of acceptable forms: e.g. book form, loose-leaf binder or computer records.

- The accounting records should be up to date, should be readily available, and should provide the basic information from which the financial position can be ascertained, not only at the year-end, but on any selected date.

- The accounting records should contain:

  - details of all money received and expended, the date, and the nature of the receipt or expenditure; and
  - details of assets and liabilities.

- Smaller PCCs may not maintain formal ledgers to record assets and liabilities, and in such instances the requirements can generally be met by maintaining files for unpaid invoices and amounts receivable. A record of fixed assets is generally necessary to meet the accounting requirements. Some churches will maintain this record in the form of an 'inventory'. For more explanation of the fixed assets that may be held by a PCC, see Chapter 5.

Direction 5 – Comparison with accounting records

> The examiner shall compare the accounts of the charity with the accounting records in sufficient detail to provide a reasonable basis on which to decide whether the accounts are in accordance with such accounting records.

- It is necessary to compare the financial statements with the underlying accounting records to be satisfied that the accounts properly show what income the PCC has received, how it has spent its funds and, where transactions relate to restricted or endowment funds, that these have been properly recorded and identified in the accounts.

- Where prepared on an accruals basis, all balances in the financial statements will need to be compared with the trial balance, analysed cash book or any nominal ledger maintained.

- Where financial statements are prepared on a receipts and payments basis a direct comparison with the cash records of the PCC should be carried out if no nominal ledger is kept.

- Test checks will also be necessary of the posting of entries from books of prime entry (e.g. cash book, petty cash book, services or offerings register, etc.) to any nominal ledger and/or to the trial balance itself. Similar checks are also necessary even where accounting records are maintained by using computer accounting packages as the internal integrity of such packages cannot be assumed.

- A review of bank reconciliations, and any control accounts prepared, will provide a useful check as to the completeness and accuracy of postings from books of prime entry.

- There is no requirement for accounting entries to be checked against source documents (e.g. invoices, Gift Aid records etc.) unless concerns arise during the course of the examination which cannot be resolved by seeking explanations.

- While the PCC is responsible for the preparation of financial statements, in some parishes the examiner may also prepare financial statements on behalf of the PCC. The preparation of financial statements will not generally impinge on the examiner's independence provided that:

  - the requirements of the Charity Commission's Directions have been met;
  - the accounting records (the books of prime entry) have been maintained by another person; and
  - the examiner has had no direct involvement in the day-to-day management or administration of the PCC.

Direction 6 – Analytical procedures

> The examiner shall carry out analytical procedures to identify unusual items or disclosures in the accounts. Where concerns arise from these procedures, the examiner must seek an explanation from the charity trustees. If, after following such procedures, the examiner has reason to believe that in any respect the accounts may be materially misstated then additional procedures, including verification of the asset, liability, incoming resource or application, must be carried out.

- It is important that the examiner looks carefully at the financial statements to see if they reveal any unusual items, unexpected fluctuations, or inconsistencies with other financial information. This procedure is called analytical review. Steps taken would normally include:

  - comparing the financial statements with those for comparable prior periods;

  - comparing the financial statements with any budgets or forecasts that have been produced;

  - considering whether incoming resources and the application of resources are consistent with known fund-raising sources, activities, and the objectives of the PCC. It is important to have obtained a proper understanding of the nature of the PCC's activities and affairs for this aspect of the review to be successful;

- considering whether the current assets and liabilities disclosed are consistent with the scale and type of activities undertaken;

- considering whether fixed-asset investments are producing an income consistent with their size and nature; and

- considering whether the tangible fixed assets are consistent with the scale and type of activity undertaken by the PCC.

● Where analytical review procedures identify any unusual item, unexpected fluctuation or inconsistency, then explanations should be sought from the PCC.

● If the explanations provided by the PCC do not satisfy the examiner, then additional procedures will be necessary. Such procedures may include:

- comparison of amounts of planned giving with Gift Aid declarations held or Envelope Scheme records;

- direct confirmation from grant makers of amounts remitted to the PCC;

- physical inspection of a tangible fixed asset;

- verification of title to an asset (e.g. an investment certificate or title deeds);

- inspection of third-party documentary evidence (e.g. invoice, contract or agreement) to verify any expense or liability or to confirm an amount of income received or receivable;

- third-party certification of a bank balance, or other asset held, including the custody of investment certificates; and

- checking of a post year-end receipt or payment to confirm recoverability of a debt or the amount of a liability.

● A comprehensive list of analytical procedures, and of additional procedures where concerns arise, is beyond the scope of this guidance, and will to an extent be an area in which the examiner will need to exercise judgement and draw on experience.

Direction 7 – Form and content of financial statements

> The examiner shall carry out such procedures as the examiner considers necessary to provide a reasonable basis on which to decide whether or not the accounts prepared under section 132 of the Charities Act 2011 comply with the form and content requirements of the Charities (Accounts and Reports) Regulations 2008 including their preparation in accordance with the methods and principles set out in the Statement of Recommended Practice: Accounting and Reporting by Charities 2005 (the SORP)

● Accruals basis

Where financial statements are prepared on an accruals basis, the Regulations lay down the requirements as to the form and content of such financial statements.

The examiner should be conversant with the Regulations as to the form and content of PCC financial statements and should examine the financial statements in sufficient detail to ensure compliance with these Regulations (but without regard to their requirement for a 'true and fair view' to be shown by the financial statements).

The Regulations draw heavily on the recommendations of the Statement of Recommended Practice – Accounting and Reporting by Charities 2005 (the Charities SORP).

A more detailed knowledge of the Charities SORP will be required, as the notes to the financial statements will require a statement as to whether or not they have been prepared in accordance with any applicable accounting standards and statements of recommended practice. Further details for financial statements prepared on an accruals basis are provided in Chapters 4 and 5 and guidance for any group accounts in Chapter 7.

• Receipts and Payments basis

The Regulations do not specify the form and content of financial statements prepared on a receipts and payments basis. The Charity Commission created the Charity SORP (the Accounting and Reporting by Charities: Statement of Recommended Practice), to give clear guidelines on what information to keep and what reports to produce to meet our legal obligations. The Church of England has adopted the SORP as its standard basis for annual financial reporting by parishes.

Guidance on the form and content of such financial statements can be found in the Receipts and Payments Guide. While this publication sets out best practice for the format of such financial statements, there is no requirement for the examiner to carry out specific procedures to ensure compliance with that guidance.

Direction 8 – Accounting policies, estimates and judgements

When financial statements are prepared on an accruals basis, the examiner shall review the accounting policies adopted and consider their consistency with the Statement of Recommended Practice: Accounting and Reporting by Charities (the SORP) and their appropriateness to the activities of the charity. The examiner must also consider and review any significant estimate or judgement that has been made in preparing the financial statements.

• Accruals basis

The accounting policies adopted, and also any estimates or judgements made in preparing the financial statements, may have a material effect on both the financial activities and state of affairs disclosed by the financial statements. Such matters, therefore, require careful consideration by the examiner.

The examiner should be satisfied that financial statements are prepared on a basis consistent with the going concern assumption and the accruals accounting concepts and that the accounting policies adopted conform to these concepts. The accounting policies adopted should be those that are most appropriate to the activities of the PCC and ensure a relevant, reliable, comparable and understandable financial statements presentation. Model accounting policies are provided in Chapter 2.

The examiner must consider the reasonableness of any estimates or judgements where they are material to the financial statements. Matters that may require consideration include:

- the allocation of monies received to restricted or unrestricted funds;

- the inclusion of figures relating to subsidiary organisations such as fellowship groups and 'Friends' associations;

- transfers to or from designated fund accounts;

- valuation of gifts in kind;

- valuation of fixed-asset investments where no market prices exist;

- estimates resulting from transactions not being fully recorded in the accounting records; and

- where applicable, the allocation of costs between the various expenditure categories of the Statement of Financial Activities (SOFA) – see Chapter 4.

- whether there are any events occurring after the balance sheet date which have a material effect on the financial statements under review.

These could include:

- any income anticipated and accrued in the financial statements at the year end but which has proved irrecoverable;

- the discovery of an error or fraud;

- the crystallisation of any liability;

- the repayment of a grant or donation received; or

- a valuation of a property indicating a diminution of value.

- **Receipts and Payments basis**

The only fundamental accounting concept which applies to financial statements prepared on a receipts and payments basis is that of consistency. Accounting policies and judgemental issues have less relevance since the Receipts and Payments account is simply a factual record of money actually received and expended. The Statement of Assets and Liabilities is a straightforward schedule of information. This direction therefore does not apply to such accounts, unless other examination procedures have given rise to concerns that need to be addressed in this way.

Direction 9 – The charity's Annual Report

> When accounts are prepared under section 132 of the Charities Act 2011 the examiner shall compare the accounts to any financial references in the charity's Annual Report, identifying any major inconsistencies and consider the significance such matters will have on a proper and accurate understanding of the charity's accounts.

- If accounts are prepared on the receipts and payments basis under section 133 of the Charities Act 2011 there is no statutory requirement for the examiner to consider the PCC's Annual Report. However, for good practice, it is recommended that the examiner should review the Annual Report with particular attention to ensuring that any financial information in the report is in agreement with the financial statements.

- The PCC's Annual Report provides a report of the PCC's activities during the financial year. The Regulations specify the information that is to be contained in such reports. Guidance on this is given in Chapter 6.

- Procedures should be directed at identifying inconsistencies with the financial statements which are misleading or which contradict the financial information contained in the financial statements.

- Where inconsistencies are identified which may have a significant effect on the proper understanding of the financial statements, these should be drawn to the attention of the PCC. If no appropriate amendment is made to the Annual Report, then details of the matter should be provided in the examiner's report.

Direction 10 – Examiner's report

> The examiner shall review and assess all conclusions drawn from the evidence obtained from the examination and consider the implications on the report to be made under Regulation 31 of the 2008 Regulations. If the examiner has cause to make a positive statement on any matter arising from the provisions of Regulation 31(h) or 31(i), or to make a statement on any matter arising from the provisions of Regulation 31(j), then the examiner must ensure so far as is practicable that the report gives a clear explanation of the matter and of its financial effects on the financial statements presented.

- The requirements as to the form and content of the examiner's report are set out in the Charities (Accounts and Reports) Regulations 2008. An illustrative example is included below. The examiner needs to consider carefully the conclusions drawn from the procedures undertaken in accordance with the Commission's directions, and the impact of these conclusions on the examiner's report.

- In providing the examination report the examiner must state whether or not any matter has come to their attention, in connection with the examination, which gives reasonable cause to believe that in any material respect:

- accounting records have not been kept in accordance with section 130 of the Charities Act 2011 and with the Church Accounting Regulations 2006

- the financial statements do not accord with the accounting records; or

- where the accounts are prepared on an accruals basis under section 132 of the Charities Act 2011, those accounts do not comply with the requirements of the Charities (Accounts and Reports) Regulations 2008 setting out the form and content of charity accounts.

- Where any of the above concerns have been identified there should be a clear explanation of the nature of the failure and its effects on the financial statements. If the financial effects cannot be ascertained due to uncertainty, the nature of the uncertainty should be explained.

- If the concern relates to non-compliance with the Regulations as to the form and content of financial statements, this should be raised with the PCC to seek the necessary amendment to the financial statements.

- The examiner is also required to state whether or not any matter has come to their attention in connection with the examination to which, in the examiner's opinion, attention should be drawn in the report to enable a proper understanding of the financial statements to be reached. This is only likely to relate to significant matters.

- Where such matters have come to the attention of the examiner, they should be brought to the attention of the PCC with a view to seeking an amendment or adjustment to the financial statements. If concerns remain the matter should be addressed in the examiner's report. The matter concerned should be fully explained together with the effects on the financial statements.

- There is also a requirement to provide a statement if the following matters have become apparent to the examiner during the course of the examination:

  - there has been any material expenditure or action which appears not to be in accordance within the objects of the PCC as set out in the Parochial Church Councils (Powers) Measure or any special trusts of the PCC;

  - the financial statements are inconsistent in any material respect with the annual report of the PCC;

  - there has been any failure in the provision of information and explanations by any past or present officer of the PCC that is considered necessary for the examination.

- An understanding of the objectives and proper activities of the PCC should enable an examiner to recognise a material expenditure or action which does not appear to be in accordance with such objects. While an immaterial technical breach would not concern the examiner, material actions or expenditure contrary to the objects of the PCC would be a major concern. The examiner need not carry out specific procedures to identify such breaches, but must include a statement on them in the report where they have been identified.

- Any major inconsistency between the financial statements and the PCC's annual report may give rise to misunderstanding. This should be brought to the attention of the PCC with a view to the amendment of the discrepancy. Where concerns still exist after any amendments are made this must be stated in the examiner's report.

Example Independent Examiner's Report

Independent Examiner's Report to the members/trustees of St Ledger's Church, Ambridge, Parochial Church Council.

I report on the accounts for the year ended 31st December 2012 which are set out on pages 6 to 8.

Respective responsibilities of the Trustees and Independent Examiner

The charity's trustees consider that an audit is not required for this year under section 144(2) of the Charities Act 2011 (the 2011 Act) and that an independent examination is needed.

It is my responsibility to

- examine the accounts under section 145 of the 2011 Act;

- follow the procedures laid down in the General Directions given by the Charity Commissioners section 145(5)(b) of the 2011 Act; and

- state whether particular matters have come to my attention.

Basis of Independent Examiner's Statement

My examination was carried out in accordance with the General Directions given by the Charity Commission.

An examination includes a review of the accounting records kept by the charity and a comparison of the accounts presented with those records. It also includes consideration of any unusual items or disclosures in the accounts, and seeking explanations from the management committee concerning any such matters. The procedures undertaken do not provide all the evidence that would be required in a full audit, and consequently I do not express an audit opinion on the accounts.

Independent Examiner's Statement

In connection with my examination, no matters have come to my attention

1. which give me reasonable cause to believe that in any material respect the requirements

   - to keep accounting records in accordance with s.130 of the 2011 Act; or

   - to prepare accounts which accord with these accounting records have not been met; or

2. to which, in my opinion, attention should be drawn in order to enable a proper understanding of the accounts to be reached.

Sarah Temple, MCIE

18 Church Close,

Ambleforth

16 March 2013

Reports to the Charity Commission and other regulatory bodies

- If the examiner finds a problem that causes concern, they should be clear in their mind what the problem is. First they should clarify matters with the treasurer and, if appropriate, the minister and the churchwardens, who are the Bishop's officers in the parish. If the matter is legal or technical they should talk to an appropriate professional person and, if necessary, someone at the local diocesan office. If they are being obstructed in their work, for example not being given access to documents, they should contact the Archdeacon or the diocesan office.

- If, having established the problem, the examiner is still concerned, there are a number of alternative courses of action depending on the scale of the problem:

  - The examiner can report the matter to the PCC separately, probably in the form of a letter – often called a 'management letter' when used by professional auditors. The letter will need to be carefully drafted to make it intelligible and tactful and it is good practice to discuss it with the treasurer and include their comments. The treasurer should ensure this is discussed at a PCC meeting. This would cover smaller concerns that the examiner might have, such as a poor or inefficient accounting system or areas where control is weak or, more likely, not clearly evidenced. Such a letter should help the PCC improve its administration and control.

  - The examiner may feel they have to make a qualified report attached to the financial statements. There may be an occasion where this is only a question of emphasis, for example where the PCC might be facing significant legal exposure from a court case which is yet to be resolved. Normally, however, a qualified report would be a serious matter and the independent examiner would be wise to seek advice from professional colleagues and the diocesan office before issuing the report. However, should the situation arise, the examiner must determine the content of their report and how their concerns are to be expressed.

  - The examiner may feel concerned that there are more serious problems, for example possible minor fraud or the inappropriate use of PCC funds (such as the incorrect use of a restricted fund) which need to be resolved prior to considering issuing a report. These concerns should be raised with the minister and churchwardens. If the examiner finds that they are unwilling or unable to take action then they should consider exploring the problem with the Archdeacon responsible for the parish.

  - At the most serious level would be a matter that the independent examiner has to report to the Charity Commission under the Charities Act (section 156) This places a duty upon an independent examiner to make a report to the Charity Commission where, in the course of their examination, they have identified a matter which relates to the activities or affairs of the PCC which the examiner has reasonable cause to believe is likely to be of material significance for the exercise of the Commission's supervisory powers.

- An independent examiner should ensure that the appropriate Archdeacon receives a copy of any qualified or Charity Commission report. If the examiner suspects that a crime may have been committed (e.g. fraud) then, in conjunction with the Archdeacon, minister and churchwardens, consideration should be given as to whether the matter should be reported to the police.

Audit/Independent examination comparison

Procedure	Audit	Independent examination
Opinion required as to whether financial statements show a true and fair view	Yes	No
Level of assurance given	High, positive	Moderate, negative
Check accounting records to establish entitlement to independent examination instead of audit	n/a	Yes
Obtain understanding of the PCC's organisation, accounting system, activities and nature of its assets, liabilities, incoming resources and application of resources in order to plan appropriate procedures	Yes	Yes
Record the procedures carried out and document matters that are important to support conclusions reached or statements provided in the report	Yes	Yes
Consideration of accounting records (i.e. that they are in accordance with section 130 of the Charities Act 2011)	Yes	Yes
Analytical review	Yes	Yes
Substantive testing, e.g. vouching source documents, physical inspection of fixed assets, obtaining bank confirmation of balances, inspection of investment certificates etc.	Yes	No – unless the analytical review shows unusual items for which the PCC cannot give satisfactory explanations
Review financial statements for conformity with applicable rules on form and content	Yes	Yes
Considering conformity with fundamental accounting concepts and the going concern assumption. Consider any significant estimate or judgement made in preparing the financial statements	Yes	Yes – in case of accruals-based accounts. policies adopted by the PCC should conform to fundamental accounting concepts and be appropriate to the activities of the PCC
Post balance sheet events	Obtain sufficient appropriate evidence	Enquiry of the PCC (accruals-based accounts)
Identify and report on any major inconsistencies between any financial references in the annual report and financial statements	Yes	Yes
Obtain all information and explanations needed to carry out the scrutiny – report any failure to the PCC and other bodies (as appropriate)	Yes	Yes

Moving from Receipts and Payments to Accruals based Accounting

Introduction

The income threshold at which accruals-based accounting becomes compulsory was raised from £100,000 to £250,000 in 2009 and confirmed in the Charities Act 2011. Although this is far above the gross income level for the vast majority of PCCs there are some good reasons why a PCC might consider making the move and this Appendix sets out to demystify the accruals basis of annual accounting and explain, in simple terms, what is necessary to make the change.

Background

Over the past few decades a whole raft of accounting legislation has been issued with the objective of removing ambiguities and providing confidence in financial statements. Most recently this has taken on an international aspect as the global nature of organisations and businesses has increased. Commercial annual accounting requires, among other things, the production of a balance sheet and profit and loss account for each financial year. The balance sheet must reflect a 'true and fair view' of the value of the entity at a particular date, and the profit and loss account shows the incoming resources and expenditure that have occurred throughout the financial period, with the resultant profit/loss for the financial year. The accounting requirements for charities are no less rigorous except where annual gross income does not exceed £250,000 and the charity is not a company, when annual reporting is allowed on a simple receipts and payments basis as an unregulated 'easy option' in the public interest.

To be sure of a 'true and fair view' there are rules relating to the recognition of assets and liabilities, which are defined in those rules as rights or obligations in respect of the future transfer of 'economic benefit'. In practical terms this means that if, for example, the right to some income arises within the financial period, then it should be included as a debtor in the assets section of the balance sheet even if the cash has not yet been received. This is all subtly different from the old 'matching principle' that some readers may be familiar with, that dictated that revenues should be matched to the costs that relate to them or are incurred in generating them. A further guiding principle is that the accounts are prepared on the assumption that the entity is a 'going concern' for the foreseeable future and this affects the valuation of assets and assessment of liabilities.

As many PCCs face a challenging financial position, the need for their annual accounts to reflect the diligent and effective management of resources becomes increasingly important and accruals-based annual accounting enables the reader to see this more clearly. The inclusion of the change in the value of any investment assets is significant, as frequently PCCs are having to cash in some of these in order to pay their bills.

Application of the rules for assets and liabilities

In recognising assets as incoming resources and liabilities as resources expended, accounts-preparation adjustments need to be made to cash-accounting records. These adjustments are in respect of any amounts received or paid that relate to an event occurring in a different year. The two main areas in which this occurs are:

1. Any expenses that have been incurred but which have not yet been paid need to be shown as a liability (creditor / accrual) in the balance sheet with the other side of the entry being the expense for the period, thus indicating the true cost for the period. Examples of this might be a utility bill for December or the cost of tuning the organ just before Christmas which is paid in January; £6,200 for organ tuning in this example.

Conversely, where an expense such as insurance has been paid in advance the cost for the year is reduced by the amount relating to the next year, and is balanced with a 'prepayment' asset in the balance sheet.

Similarly the right to a Gift Aid tax repayment may exist at the year end and will need to be shown as an asset (debtor) in the balance sheet and included in the income of the current year, although it is not actually received until the next year; £2,240 in this example.

A further adjustment should be made if significant amounts of wedding fee deposits have been received for next year's weddings; such amounts should be deducted from the fee income for the year and the amount of income received in advance shown as a liability.

2.   When a significant asset such as a photocopier, that will bring benefits to the parish over several years, is purchased, it should be recognised as an asset and then its cost expensed in the accounts over its anticipated useful life by an accounting process termed depreciation. The accounting policies in the notes to the accounts must state on what basis large items are capitalised and depreciated.

Reports and terminology

Under Receipts and Payments (R&P) accounting each fund is effectively a summarised cashbook showing the 'ins and outs' of the fund, the excess of receipts over payments (or vice versa!), any transfers between differently restricted funds and the opening and closing balances on the funds in each case.

The Statement of Assets and Liabilities then lists the sum of the closing balances of all the various bank accounts (adjusted for timing differences arising from items such as cheques written at the end of the month and not yet appearing on the bank statement) which must equal the sum of the balances on the various cash funds.

Also listed (descriptively) must be any other assets such as investments and property, as well as any amounts due to the PCC such as Gift Aid recoverable and any liabilities such as an outstanding bill for the cost of the pre-Christmas organ tuning.

Note though that although listed, these other assets and liabilities are not included in the cash fund totals.

In a set of accruals-based accounts, however, a balance sheet must be produced which adds the value of all the non-cash assets and liabilities into the fund balances to give a more complete reflection of the true financial position of the PCC. You will see in the following comparison that there are two possible formats that can be used; the more detail that is included in the balance sheet the less needs to be shown in the notes to the accounts.

A comparison of the two reporting structures and associated terminology follows:

Receipts and Payments Accounts	=	Statement of Financial Activities
Receipts		Incoming Resources
Payments		Resources Expended
Excess of receipts over payments		Net incoming resources before other recognised gains and losses
Transfers between funds		Transfers between funds
N/A		Gains/(Losses) on investments and changes in the Balance Sheet value of functional fixed assets
N/A		Net movement in funds
Opening cash at bank and in hand		Fund Balances b/fwd 1 January
Closing cash at bank and in hand		Fund Balances c/fwd 31 December
Statement of Assets and Liabilities	**=**	**Balance Sheet**
Assets retained for church use		Fixed Assets – Tangible (for own use)
Investment Assets		– Investment
Other Monetary assets e.g. tax recoverable		Current Assets – Stock e.g. books for sale – Debtors e.g. tax recoverable
Deposit account		– Short term deposits
Bank current account		– Cash at bank and in hand
Liabilities		Liabilities – Creditors due less than one year – Creditors due more than one year
N/A		Parish Funds that equal the sum of all the assets less the liabilities

Making the change

A good starting point is to look thoroughly through the simple example of the Receipts & Payments accounts for St Emilion's Church on the next page and then at the accounts presented in the accrual format. See how the Balance Sheet matches both assets and liabilities to the total fund balances and see also how further details are included in the notes to the accounts.

The Opening Balance Sheet

To produce the opening balance sheet you will need to look at the previous year's statement of assets and liabilities and add the amounts* of other assets and liabilities into the calculated fund balances.

In this example:

Property with a cost value of	£59,000
+ Investments with value of	£19,500
+ Cash funds of	£21,000
= Total fund balances	£99,500 at the start of the year

(*This will be cost- based except for any investment securities/properties, for which the year-end market value (estimated if need be) is required under the Regulations.)

Note that although it is not necessary in the balance sheet to show how the comparative year values are split across the different categories of funds, it is still necessary to determine this allocation in order to calculate the opening balance on each fund.

In this example Note 4 of the R&P accounts indicates that of the £20,650 of short-term bank deposits £13,400 belongs to the restricted Church fabric fund, while the designated Organ fund forms part of the Unrestricted funds.

The Statement of Financial Activities (SOFA)

When changing the method of accounting both the current and comparative year's figures must be calculated on the same basis. For this reason it is necessary to examine the statement of assets and liabilities for the current and two preceding years and, where necessary, adjust the R&P figures to create the SOFA and its comparatives. In this example there are no 'Other Monetary Assets' or 'Liabilities' for the comparative or preceding year but if this were not the case then you would have to look back to those previous year's accounts in order to adjust the prior year figures.

The adjustments to be made in each case for the current year are:

To convert receipts to incoming resources;

Take the R&P receipt amount LESS opening debtor PLUS closing debtor

E.g. Gift Aid recoverable of £8,700 – zero + £2,240 = £10,940

To convert expenses to resources expended;

Take the R&P expense amount LESS opening liabilities PLUS closing liabilities

E.g. Organ inspection costs of zero – zero + £6,200 = £6,200 which forms part of

Church activity expenses where £64,050 – zero + £6,200 = £70,250

The example also shows where the change in the market value of the investment assets needs to be included in the calculation of the final fund balance and detailed in Note 5.

Accounting policies

The policies adopted must be noted in the case of accruals-based accounts. Refer to the examples for both St Emilion (see below) and St Ledger (see Appendix ii) for guidance on what should be included.

Note that it is important that the change in accounting basis is highlighted, both in the accounting policies section and in the financial review within the annual report.

Receipts and Payments Accounts

PAROCHIAL CHURCH COUNCIL OF ST EMILION'S CHURCH, BARCHESTER

Financial Statements for the Year Ended 31 December 2012

Receipts and Payments Accounts

	Note	Unrestricted Funds £	Restricted Funds £	Endowment Funds £	TOTAL 2012 £	TOTAL 2011 £
RECEIPTS						
Voluntary Receipts:						
Planned giving		29,400	-	-	29,400	27,200
Collections at services		9,900	-	-	9,900	10,600
All other giving/voluntary receipts	5a	2,700	5,800	-	8,500	7,050
Gift Aid recovered		8,700	-	-	8,700	8,300
		50,700	5,800	-	56,500	53,150
Activities for generating funds	5b	3,500	-	-	3,500	4,250
Investment income	5c	4,600	950	-	5,550	5,300
Church activities	5d	5,400	-	-	5,400	5,150
Total receipts		64,200	6,750	-	70,950	67,850
PAYMENTS						
Church activities:						
Diocesan parish contribution		41,500	-	-	41,500	37,050
Clergy and staffing costs		1,900	-	-	1,900	1,800
Church running expenses	5e	13,700	1,850	-	15,550	15,250
Hall running costs		1,200	-	-	1,200	1,200
Mission giving and donations	5f	2,550	1,350	-	3,900	2,550
		60,850	3,200	-	64,050	57,850
Costs of generating funds		500	-	-	500	500
Total payments		61,350	3,200	-	64,550	58,350
Excess of Receipts over Payments		2,850	3,550	-	6,400	9,500
Transfers between funds	4	(100)	100	-	-	-
		2,750	3,650	-	6,400	9,500
Cash at bank and in hand at 1 January		7,600	13,400	-	21,000	11,500
Cash at bank and in hand at 31 December		10,350	17,050	-	27,400	21,000

Statement of Assets and Liabilities

	Note	Unrestricted Funds £	Restricted Funds £	Endowment Funds £	TOTAL 2012 £	TOTAL 2011 £
Cash Funds						
Bank Current Account		300	-	-	300	350
Deposit Funds		10,050	17,050		27,100	20,650
		10,350	17,050	-	27,400	21,000
Other Monetary Assets						
Gift Aid recoverable		2,240	-	-	2,240	-
Investment Assets						
Investment Fund shares at market value	3	-	-	20,000	20,000	19,500
Assets retained for church use	2	59,000	-	-	59,000	59,000
Liabilities						
Organ cleaning/tune		6,200	-	-	6,200	-

Notes

1. The financial statements of the PCC have been prepared in accordance with the Church Accounting Regulations 2006 using the Receipts and Payments basis.

2. Fixed assets retained for church use is the freehold house at 36 Church Street, purchased 5 November 1984, at cost.

3. The Endowment fund, a donation in 1999 by R. H. Smith, has to be retained as a capital fund, but the income is for ordinary church purposes. It is invested in CCLA Church of England Investment fund shares.

4. The movements in designated and restricted funds during the year were:

	Bal b/fwd	Receipts	Payments	Transfer	Bal c/fwd
Designated					
Organ fund	3,300	-	-	2,000	5,300
Restricted					
Church fabric (inc tower)	13,400	5,050	1,400	-	17,050
Southern Africa Famine Appeal	-	1,350	1,350	-	-
Flower fund	-	350	450	100	-
	13,400	6,750	3,200	100	17,050

The transfer to the Organ fund was from ordinary unrestricted funds to meet the balance of the cleaning/tuning costs.

The Fabric fund represents accumulated donations and appeals for fabric maintenance, which can only be spent for that purpose.

The Southern Africa Famine Appeal represents funds raised by the Mission and Evangelism Committee to relieve poverty and hardship in the recent famine in Southern Africa.

The Flower fund represents a donation from a parishioner to be spent on Easter lilies in memory of her recently deceased mother.

The cost of the flowers is included in costs of services. A further £100 was designated from the general fund to meet the full cost of lilies.

5. Further Analysis of Receipts and Payments Accounts

	Note	Unrestricted Funds £	Restricted Funds £	Endowment Funds £	TOTAL 2012 £	TOTAL 2011 £
Receipts						
a) **All other giving/voluntary receipts**						
Donations		1,700	5,800	-	7,500	7,050
Legacy		1,000	-	-	1,000	–
		2,700	5,800	-	8,500	7,050
b) **Activities for generating funds:**						
Parish magazine – advertising		1,100	-	-	1,100	1,050
Summer fete and Christmas bazaar		2,400	-	-	2,400	2,500
Rummage sales		-	-	-	-	700
		3,500	-	-	3,500	4,250
c) **Investment income:**						
Dividends on CBF Investment Funds		500	-	-	500	500
Bank and CBF Deposit Fund interest		400	950	-	1,350	1,100
Rent – temporary let on curate's house		3,700	-	-	3,700	3,700
		4,600	950	-	5,550	5,300
d) **Church activities:**						
Fees for weddings and funerals		400	-	-	400	300
Parish magazine income – sales		1,100	-	-	1,100	1,050
Church Centre lettings – local community use		3,900	-	-	3,900	3,800
		5,400	-	-	5,400	5,150
Payments						
e) **Church running expenses:**						
Sunday School teacher training		1,000	-	-	1,000	-
Organ inspection		-	-	-	-	150
Costs of services		2,600	450	-	3,050	2,100
Printing and stationery		1,100	-	-	1,100	1,200
Church building running expenses		4,700	-	-	4,700	4,800
Parish magazine printing		1,800	-	-	1,800	1,800
Church repairs and maintenance		2,500	1,400	-	3,900	5,200
		13,700	1,850	-	15,550	15,250
f) **Mission giving and donations**						
CMS		1,200	-	-	1,200	1,200
Southern Africa Famine appeal		1,350	1,350	-	2,700	-
Earthquake appeal		-	-	-	-	1,350
		2,550	1,350	-	3,900	2,550

Accrual accounts

PAROCHIAL CHURCH COUNCIL OF ST EMILION'S CHURCH, BARCHESTER

Financial Statements for the Year Ended 31 December 2012

Statement of Financial Activities

	Note	Unrestricted Funds	Restricted Funds	Endowment Funds	TOTAL 2012	TOTAL 2011
		£	£	£	£	£
Incoming Resources						
Voluntary income	2(a)	52,940	5,800	-	58,740	53,150
Activities for generating funds	2(b)	3,500	-	-	3,500	4,250
Investment income	2(c)	4,600	950	-	5,550	5,300
Church activities	2(d)	5,400	-	-	5,400	5,150
Total Incoming Resources		66,440	6,750	-	73,190	67,850
Resources Expended						
Church activities	3(a)	67,050	3,200	-	70,250	57,850
Costs of generating funds		500	-	-	500	500
Total Resources Expended		67,550	3,200	-	70,750	58,350
Net Incoming Resources before transfers		(1,110)	3,550	-	2,440	9,500
Transfers between funds	4	(100)	100	-	-	-
Net Incoming Resources before other recognised gains/(losses)		(1,210)	3,650	-	2,440	9,500
Revaluation gains on investments	5	-	-	500	500	-
Net Movement in Funds		(1,210)	3,650	500	2,940	9,500
Balances b/fwd 1 January		66,600	13,400	19,500	99,500	90,000
Balances c/fwd 31 December	9(a)	65,390	17,050	20,000	102,440	99,500

Balance Sheet at 31 December 2012 – Option 1

	Note	Unrestricted Funds £	Restricted Funds £	Endowment Funds £	TOTAL 2012 £	TOTAL 2011 £
Fixed Assets						
Tangible	6	59,000	-	-	59,000	59,000
Investments	5	-	-	20,000	20,000	19,500
		59,000	-	20,000	79,000	78,500
Current Assets						
Receivables and Prepayments	7	2,240	-	-	2,240	-
Short-term deposits		10,050	17,050	-	27,100	20,650
Cash at bank and in hand		300	-	-	300	350
		12,590	17,050	-	29,640	21,000
Current Liabilities						
Payables falling due < 1 year	8	6,200	-	-	6,200	-
Net Current Assets		6,390	17,050	-	23,440	21,000
Total Net Assets	9b	65,390	17,050	20,000	102,440	99,500
Parish Funds		65,390	17,050	20,000	102,440	99,500

Balance Sheet at 31 December 2012 – Option 2

	Note	2012 £	2011 £
Fixed Assets			
Tangible	6	59,000	59,000
Investments	5	20,000	19,500
		79,000	78,500
Current Assets			
Receivables and Prepayments	7	2,240	-
Short-term deposits		27,100	20,650
Cash at bank and in hand		300	350
		29,640	21,000
Current Liabilities			
Payables falling due < 1 year	8	6,200	-
Net Current Assets		23,440	21,000
Total Net Assets	9(b)	102,440	99,500
Parish Funds			
Unrestricted		65,390	66,600
Restricted		17,050	13,400
Endowment		20,000	19,500
		102,440	99,500

Notes

1.　Accounting policies

Basis of financial statements

The financial statements have been prepared under the Church Accounting Regulations 2006 in accordance with applicable accounting standards and the current Statement of Recommended Practice, Accounting and Reporting by Charities (SORP 2005).

The financial statements have been prepared under the historical cost convention except for investment assets, which are shown at market value. The financial statements include all transactions, assets and liabilities for which the PCC is responsible in law. They do not include the accounts of church groups that owe their main affiliation to another body, nor those that are informal gatherings of church members.

This is the first year that the accounts have been prepared using the accrual accounting method and this has resulted in the significant year-on-year variation in the gift aid recovered income and organ inspection costs.

Fund accounting

Endowment Funds are funds, the capital of which must be retained either permanently or at the PCC's discretion; the income derived from the endowment is to be used either as restricted or unrestricted income funds depending upon the purpose for which the endowment was established in the first place.

Restricted Funds comprise (a) income from endowments which is to be expended only on the restricted purposes intended by the donor, and (b) revenue donations or grants for a specific PCC activity intended by the donor. Where these funds have unspent balances, interest on their pooled investment is apportioned to the individual funds on an average balance basis.

Unrestricted Funds are income funds which are to be spent on the PCC's general purposes.

Designated funds are general funds set aside by the PCC for use in the future. Project funds are designated for particular projects for administration purposes only. Funds designated as invested in fixed assets for the PCC's own use are abated in line with those assets' annual depreciation charges in the SOFA. Designated funds remain unrestricted and the PCC will move any surplus to other general funds.

Incoming resources

Planned giving, collections and similar donations are recognised when received. Tax refunds are recognised when the incoming resource to which they relate is received. Grants and legacies are accounted for when the PCC is entitled to the use of the resources, their ultimate receipt is considered reasonably certain and the amounts due are readily quantifiable. Dividends are accounted for when declared receivable, interest as and when accrued by the payer. All incoming resources are accounted for gross.

Resources expended

Grants and donations are accounted for when paid over, or when awarded, if that award creates a binding or constructive obligation on the PCC. The diocesan parish share expected to be paid over is accounted for when due. All other expenditure is generally recognised when it is incurred and is accounted for gross.

Fixed assets

Consecrated and benefice property is not included in the accounts in accordance with s.10(2)(a) and (c) of the Charities Act 2011.

Movable church furnishings held by the vicar and churchwardens on special trust for the PCC and which require a faculty for disposal are inalienable property, listed in the church's inventory, which can be inspected (at any reasonable time). For anything acquired prior to 2000 there is insufficient cost information available and therefore such assets are not valued in the financial statements. Subsequently no individual item has cost more than £1,000 so all such expenditure has been written off when incurred.

No cost information is available for the curate's house so it is included at a deemed cost being its 1994 valuation of £65,000 (including £15,000 estimated freehold land value). The building is being depreciated at £1,000 per annum with effect from 2003 on the basis of its expected useful life of 50 years.

Equipment used within the church premises is depreciated on a straight-line basis over four years. Individual items of equipment with a purchase price of £500 or less are written off when the asset is acquired.

No depreciation is provided as the currently estimated residual value of the property (discounted for monetary inflation since it's capitalisation) is not less than its carrying value and the remaining useful life of the building currently exceeds 50 years, so that any depreciation charges would be immaterial. If the carrying value of the building looks greater than it's current value on this basis, an impairment review would be carried out and any resultant loss included in expenditure for the year.

Investments are valued at market value at 31 December.

2. Incoming resources

		Unrestricted Funds £	Restricted Funds £	Endowment Funds £	TOTAL 2012 £	TOTAL 2011 £
a)	Voluntary Income					
	Planned giving	29,400	-	-	29,400	27,200
	Collections at services	9,900	-	-	9,900	10,600
	Donations	1,700	5,800	-	7,500	7,050
	Legacy	1,000	-	-	1,000	-
	Gift Aid recovered	10,940	-	-	10,940	8,300
		52,940	5,800	-	58,740	53,150
b)	Activities for generating funds:					
	Parish magazine – advertising	1,100	-	-	1,100	1,050
	Summer fete and Christmas bazaar	2,400	-	-	2,400	2,500
	Rummage sales	-	-	-	-	700
		3,500	-	-	3,500	4,250
c)	Investment income:					
	Dividends on CBF Investment Funds	500	-	-	500	500
	Bank and CBF Deposit Fund interest	400	950	-	1,350	1,100
	Rent – temporary let on curate's house	3,700	-	-	3,700	3,700
		4,600	950	-	5,550	5,300
d)	Church activities:					
	Fees for weddings and funerals	400	-	-	400	300
	Parish magazine income – sales	1,100	-	-	1,100	1,050
	Church Centre lettings – local community use	3,900	-	-	3,900	3,800
		5,400	-	-	5,400	5,150
	Total Incoming Resources	66,440	6,750	-	73,190	67,850

3. Resources expended

		Funds	Unrestricted Funds £	Restricted Funds £	Endowment 2012 £	TOTAL 2011 £	FUNDS £
a)	**Church activity expenses**						
	Mission giving and donations						
	CMS		1,200	-	-	1,200	1,200
	Southern Africa Famine appeal		1,350	1,350	-	2,700	-
	Earthquake appeal		-	-	-	-	1,350
			2,550	1,350	-	3,900	2,550
	Diocesan parish contribution		41,500	-	-	41,500	37,050
	Clergy and staffing costs		1,900	-	-	1,900	1,800
	Sunday School teacher training		1,000	-	-	1,000	-
	Organ inspection		6,200	-	-	6,200	150
	Costs of services		2,600	450	-	3,050	2,100
	Printing and stationery		1,100	-	-	1,100	1,200
	Church building running expenses		4,700	-	-	4,700	4,800
	Parish magazine printing		1,800	-	-	1,800	1,800
	Church repairs and maintenance		2,500	1,400	-	3,900	5,200
	Hall running costs		1,200	-	-	1,200	1,200
			67,050	3,200	-	70,250	57,850

4. Transfers between funds

The transfer to the designated Organ fund was from ordinary unrestricted funds to meet the balance of the clean/tune costs.

The transfer to the restricted Flower fund was from ordinary unrestricted funds to meet the balance of the cost of the Easter lilies.

5. Investments

	Market value 1st January	Purchases	Disposals	Market value Revaluation	Market value 31st December
CCLA Investment:	£	£	£	£	£
245.9 shares in a/c 1234S	19,500	–	–	500	20,000

6. Tangible assets

This comprises the freehold house at 36 Church Street, purchased 5 November 1984, and shown at cost. It is retained for church use.

7. Accounts receivable

	2012	2011
Gift Aid recoverable	£	£
	2,240	-

8. Accounts payable

	2012	2011
Organ cleaning/tune	£	£
	6,200	-

9. Funds

(a) The movements in designated and restricted funds during the year were:

	1 Jan	Receipts	Payments	Transfer	31 Dec
Designated	£	£	£	£	£
Organ fund	3,300	-	-	2,000	5,300
Restricted					
Church fabric (inc tower)	13,400	5,050	1,400	-	17,050
Southern Africa Famine Appeal	-	1,350	1,350	-	-
Flower fund	-	350	450	100	-
	13,400	6,750	3,200	100	17,050

(b) The allocation of assets across the funds at the year end were:

[NB This is only required with Option 2 Balance Sheet]	Fixed Assets	Current Assets	Current Liabilities	Net Assets
	£	£	£	£
Unrestricted – General	59,000	7,290	6,200	60,090
Unrestricted – Designated				
Organ fund	-	5,300	-	5,300
Restricted				
Church fabric (inc tower)	-	17,050	-	17,050
Southern Africa Famine Appeal	-	-	-	-
Flower fund	-	-	-	-
Endowment R. H. Smith	20,000	-	-	20,000
Total	79,000	29,640	6,200	102,440

The Fabric fund represents accumulated donations and appeals for fabric maintenance, which can only be spent for that purpose.

The Southern Africa Famine Appeal represents funds raised by the Mission and Evangelism Committee to relieve poverty and hardship in the recent famine in Southern Africa.

The Flower fund represents a donation from a parishioner to be spent on Easter lilies in memory of her recently deceased mother. The cost of the flowers is included in costs of services.

The Endowment fund, a donation in 1999 by R. H. Smith, has to be retained as a capital fund, but the income is for ordinary church purposes. It is invested in CCLA Church of England Investment fund shares.

Example Accrual Accounts

PAROCHIAL CHURCH COUNCIL OF ST LEDGER, AMBRIDGE

STATEMENT OF FINANCIAL ACTIVITIES

For the year ending 31 December 2012

	Note	Unrestricted Funds £	Restricted Funds £	Endowment Funds £	TOTAL 2012 £	TOTAL 2011 £
INCOMING RESOURCES						
Voluntary income	2(a)	160,400	216,750	-	377,150	148,750
Activities for generating funds	2(b)	10,000	-	-	10,000	4,250
Income from investments	2(c)	7,450	2,500	-	9,950	8,800
Church activities	2(d)	15,800	-	-	15,800	13,150
TOTAL INCOMING RESOURCES		193,650	219,250	-	412,900	174,950
RESOURCES EXPENDED						
Church activities	3(a)	154,300	244,275	-	398,575	161,275
Cost of generating voluntary income	3(b)	550	1,250	-	1,800	500
Governance Costs	3(c)	950	-	-	950	675
TOTAL RESOURCES EXPENDED		155,800	245,525	-	401,325	162,450
NET INCOMING RESOURCES BEFORE TRANSFERS		37,850	(26,275)	-	11,575	12,500
GROSS TRANSFERS BETWEEN FUNDS	5	(19,000)	19,000	-	-	-
NET INCOMING RESOURCES BEFORE OTHER RECOGNISED GAINS AND LOSSES		18,850	(7,275)	-	11,575	12,500
OTHER RECOGNISED GAINS						
Gains on investment assets:	6(b) & 7(a)	5,455	1,050	245	6,750	500
NET MOVEMENT IN FUNDS		24,305	(6,225)	245	18,325	13,000
Balances b/fwd 1 January 2012	9	58,935	14,000	2,250	75,185	62,185
Balances c/fwd 31 December 2012	10	83,240	7,775	2,495	93,510	75,185

The notes on pages 3 to 7 form part of this account.

PAROCHIAL CHURCH COUNCIL OF ST LEDGER, AMBRIDGE

BALANCE SHEET AT 31 DECEMBER 2012

	Notes	2012 £	2011 £
FIXED ASSETS			
Tangible	6(a)	34,000	37,000
Investments	6(b)	13,625	14,500
		47,625	51,500
CURRENT ASSETS			
Stock		150	150
Investments	7(a)	24,060	15,000
Debtors and prepayments	7(b)	9,675	4,000
Short term deposits		11,000	8,000
Cash at bank and in hand		4,200	1,985
		49,085	29,135
LIABILITIES			
Creditors – amounts falling due within one year	8	2,700	4,450
NET CURRENT ASSETS / (LIABILITIES)		46,385	24,685
TOTAL ASSETS LESS CURRENT LIABILITIES		94,010	76,185
Creditors – amounts falling due after one year		500	1,000
TOTAL NET ASSETS		93,510	75,185
PARISH FUNDS			
Unrestricted	10	83,240	58,935
Restricted	10	7,775	14,000
Endowment	10	2,495	2,250
		93,510	75,185

Approved by the Parochial Church Council on 1 March 2013 and signed on its behalf by: The Revd James Colossae (PCC chairman), Mr David Jones (Vice Chairman and Church Warden)

The notes on pages 3 to 7 form part of these accounts.

PAROCHIAL CHURCH COUNCIL OF ST LEDGER, AMBRIDGE

NOTES TO THE FINANCIAL STATEMENTS For the year ended 31 December 2012

1. ACCOUNTING POLICIES

Basis of financial statements

The financial statements have been prepared under the Church Accounting Regulations 2006 in accordance with applicable accounting standards and the current Statement of Recommended Practice Accounting and Reporting by Charities (SORP 2005).

The financial statements have been prepared under the historical cost convention except for investment assets, which are shown at market value. The financial statements include all transactions, assets and liabilities for which the PCC is responsible in law. They do not include the accounts of church groups that owe their affiliation to another body, nor those that are informal gatherings of church members.

Fund accounting

Endowment funds are funds, the capital of which must be retained either permanently or at the PCC's discretion; the income derived from the endowment is to be used either as restricted or unrestricted income funds depending upon the purpose for which the endowment was established in the first place.

Restricted funds comprise (a) income from endowments which is to be expended only on the restricted purposes intended by the donor and (b) revenue donations or grants for a specific PCC activity intended by the donor. Where these funds have unspent balances, interest on their pooled investment is apportioned to the individual funds on an average balance basis.

Unrestricted funds are income funds which are to be spent on the PCC's general purposes.

Designated funds are general funds set aside by the PCC for use in the future. Project funds are designated for particular projects for administration purposes only. Funds designated as invested in fixed assets for the PCC's own use abated in line with assets' annual depreciation charges in the SOFA. Designated funds remain unrestricted and the PCC will move any surplus to other general funds.

Incoming resources

Planned giving, collections and similar donations are recognised when received. Tax refunds are recognised when the the incoming resource to which they relate is received. Grants and legacies are accounted for when the PCC is entitled to the use of the resources, their ultimate receipt is considered reasonably certain and the amounts due are reliably. quantifiable. Dividends are accounted for when declared receivable, interest as and when accrued by the payer. All incoming resources are accounted for gross.

PAROCHIAL CHURCH COUNCIL OF ST LEDGER, AMBRIDGE

Resources expended

Grants and donations are accounted for when paid over, or when awarded, if that award creates a binding or constructive obligation on the PCC. The diocesan parish share expected to be paid over is accounted for when due.

All other expenditure is generally recognised when it is incurred and is accounted for gross.

Fixed assets

Consecrated and benefice property is not included in the accounts in accordance with s.10(2)(a) and (c) of the Charities Act 2011.

Movable church furnishings held by the vicar and churchwardens on special trust for the PCC and which require a faculty for disposal are inalienable property, listed in the church's inventory, which can be inspected (at any reasonable time). For anything acquired prior to 2000 there is insufficient cost information available and therefore such assets are not valued in the financial statements. Subsequently no individual item has cost more than £1,000 so all such expenditure has been written off when incurred.

No cost information is available for the curate's house so it is included at a deemed cost being its 1994 valuation of £65,000 (including £15,000 estimated freehold land value). The building is being depreciated at £1,000 per annum with effect from 2003 on the basis of its expected useful life of 50 years.

Equipment used within the church premises is depreciated on a straight-line basis over four years. Individual items of equipment with a purchase price of £500 or less are written off when the asset is acquired.

Investments are valued at market value at 31 December.

PAROCHIAL CHURCH COUNCIL OF ST LEDGER, AMBRIDGE

2. INCOMING RESOURCES

			Unrestricted Funds £	Restricted Funds £	Endowment Funds £	TOTAL 2012 £	TOTAL 2011 £
2(a)	**Voluntary income**						
	Planned giving:	Gift Aid donations	107,900	2,600	-	110,500	101,300
		Tax recoverable	24,050	1,500	-	25,550	23,300
		Other	3,900	-	-	3,900	-
	Collections:	(open plate)	9,900	1,600	-	11,500	10,600
	Gift days		900	-	-	900	800
	Grants:	Major structural renewal	-	162,000	-	162,000	-
	Donations, appeals, etc.		2,750	46,800	-	49,550	7,050
	Legacies		11,000	2,250	-	13,250	5,700
			160,400	216,750	-	377,150	148,750
2(b)	**Activities for generating funds**						
	Parish Magazine (advertising)		1,100	-	-	1,100	1,050
	Summer fete and Christmas bazaar		2,900	-	-	2,900	2,500
	Fund-raising		6,000	-	-	6,000	700
			10,000	-	-	10,000	4,250
2(c)	**Income from investments**						
	Dividends on CBF Investment Fund		2,850	1,550	-	4,400	4,000
	Bank and CBF Deposit Fund Interest		400	950	-	1,350	1,100
	Rent – temporary let on curate's house		4,200	-	-	4,200	3,700
			7,450	2,500	-	9,950	8,800
2(d)	**Income from church activities**						
	Fees for weddings and funerals		9,200	-	-	9,200	8,300
	Parish Magazine (sales)		2,100	-	-	2,100	1,050
	Church Centre lettings – local community use		4,500	-	-	4,500	3,800
			15,800	-	-	15,800	13,150
	Total incoming resources		193,650	219,250	-	412,900	174,950

PAROCHIAL CHURCH COUNCIL OF ST LEDGER, AMBRIDGE

3. RESOURCES EXPENDED

		Unrestricted Funds £	Restricted Funds £	Endowment Funds £	TOTAL 2012 £	TOTAL 2011 £
3(a)	**Church activities**					
	Missionary and charitable giving					
	Overseas: CMS	11,200	-	-	11,200	11,000
	South Africa Famine appeal1,500	1,350	-	2,850	-	
	Earthquake appeal	-	-	-	-	1,350
	Support of Moses Cain and Grace Cross	-	38,650	-	38,650	-
	Home: Ambridge Pensioners Club	3,500	-	-	3,500	3,000
		16,200	40,000	-	56,200	15,350
	Ministry: Diocesan parish share	91,500	-	-	91,500	87,050
	Other ministry costs	9,000	-	-	9,000	8,800
	Church running and maintenance	14,800	10,250	-	25,050	24,550
	Major repairs – structural renewal	-	189,000	-	189,000	-
	Depreciation on curate's house and church equipment	3,000	-	-	3,000	3,000
	Sunday school leader training	2,000	-	-	2,000	2,000
	Parish magazine costs	2,200	-	-	2,200	1,800
	Churchyard upkeep	5,750	-	-	5,750	5,000
	Church hall running costs	8,300	5,000	-	13,300	12,525
	Printing and stationery	1,500	25	-	1,525	1,200
	Bank charges	50	-	-	50	-
		154,300	244,275	-	398,575	161,275
3(b)	**Generation of voluntary income**					
	Stewardship costs	500	-	-	500	500
	Costs of appeals	-	1,250	-	1,250	-
	Coffee morning costs	50	-	-	50	-
		550	1,250	-	1,800	500
3(c)	**Governance Costs**					
	PCC members induction training	450	-	-	450	200
	Independent examiner's remuneration*	500	-	-	500	475
	* (fees payable to the PCC's examiner for the examination of the financial statements)	950	-	-	950	675
	TOTAL RESOURCES EXPENDED	155,800	245,525	-	401,325	162,450

PAROCHIAL CHURCH COUNCIL OF ST LEDGER, AMBRIDGE

4(a) STAFF COSTS

	2012	2011
	£	£
Wages and salaries	4,000	3,750

During the year the PCC employed an organist, gardener and church cleaner (all part-time) but no payments were large enough to attract social security costs.

4(b) PAYMENTS TO PCC MEMBERS

As the parish organist, Miss M. Joshua, who is a member of the PCC, was paid £1,000 during the year. A small immaterial portion of the expenses paid to the incumbent may have related to his services as chairman of the PCC.

No other payments or expenses were paid to any other PCC member, persons closely connected to them or related parties.

5. ANAYSIS OF TRANSFER BETWEEN FUNDS

	Unrestricted	Restricted	Total
	£	£	£
Major structural renewal	(19,000)	19,000	-

The major structural renewal appeal was started in January 2012 and completed in October 2012. The income received from grants, fundraising and appeal totalled £170,000. The expenditure was £189,000 resulting in a deficit on the restricted project of £19,000. The PCC had anticipated the need for the major repair and had designated £10,000 from general income in the previous year. The PCC approved a transfer of £19,000 from general funds to fund the deficit on the project.

6. FIXED ASSETS

6(a) Tangible (all unrestricted)

		Curate's House (Freehold)	Church equipment	Total
		£	£	£
Actual/deemed cost	At 1 January 2012	65,000	8,000	73,000
	Disposal	-	(3,000)	(3,000)
	Additions at cost	-	2,000	2,000
	At 31 December 2012	65,000	7,000	72,000
Depreciation	At 1 January 2012	34,000	2,000	36,000
	Withdrawn on disposals	-	(1,000)	(1,000)
	Charge for the year	1,000	2,000	3,000
	At 31 December 2012	35,000	3,000	38,000
	Net book value at 31 December 2012	30,000	4,000	34,000
	Net book value at 31 December 2011	31,000	6,000	37,000

PAROCHIAL CHURCH COUNCIL OF ST LEDGER, AMBRIDGE

The curate's house is shown at cost (£65,000) which is the deemed cost under FRS15 transitional provisions, under which the property's 1994 valuation has not been updated.

Church equipment comprises office equipment. A photocopier was sold during the year for £2,000; its written-down value was £2,000. It was replaced by a smaller machine, cheaper to run.

6(b) Investments

	£
Market value at 1 January 2012	14,500
Disposal	(9,170)
Purchases at cost	2,000
Net gains	6,295
Market value at 31 December 2012	13,625

At the beginning of the year, the ABC stock was sold at the carrying value for a nil gain. During the year new investments have been made at various times in the CBF Church of England Investment fund. The holding at 31 December 2012 was 3,359 shares which cost £22,105.

PAROCHIAL CHURCH COUNCIL OF ST LEDGER, AMBRIDGE

7. CURRENT ASSETS

7(a)	Investments	£
	Market value at 1 January 2012	15,000
	Purchases at cost	8,605
	Revaluation gain	455
	Market value at 31 December 2012	24,060

		2012	2011
		£	£
7(b)	**Debtors (Unrestricted funds)**		
	Tax recoverable	6,240	3,650
	Prepayments and accrued interest	2,075	200
	Other debtors	1,360	150
		9,675	4,000

		2012	2011
8.	**LIABILITIES**	£	£
	Amounts falling due in one year (Unrestricted funds)		
	Accruals for utility and other costs	1,000	1,500
	Other creditors	1,700	1,950
	Parish share	-	1,000
		2,700	4,450
	Amounts falling due after one year (Unrestricted funds)		
	Other creditors	500	1,000

9. FUNDS

The restricted funds comprise the Church Hall fund and the Mission fund. The latter represents funds raised for and grants received for the support of the mission work of Moses Cain and Grace Cross, members of the congregation working in the Far East.

The endowment fund is the Jericho bequest, which requires income to be spent on the running of the church hall.

In line with the PCC's policy, a £10,000 provision from the general income has been held in designated funds to part fund the major structural renewal project. The provision was transferred to restricted funds during 2012 upon completion of the project. At the end of 2012 the designated funds were nil.

PAROCHIAL CHURCH COUNCIL OF ST LEDGER, AMBRIDGE

Fund movements	Church hall	Mission	Church Structural Renewal	Total
	£	£	£	£
Balance at 1 January 2012	12,975	1,025	-	14,000
Incoming resources	11,325	37,925	170,000	219,250
Resources expended	(16,525)	(40,000)	(189,000)	(245,525)
Investment gains	-	1,050	-	1,050
Transfer	-	-	19,000	19,000
Balance at 31 December 2012	7,775	-	-	7,775

10. ANALYSIS OF NET ASSETS

BY FUND	Unrestricted Funds	Restricted Funds	Endowment Funds	TOTAL 2012
	£	£	£	£
Tangible fixed assets	34,000	-	-	34,000
Investment fixed assets	3,355	7,775	2,495	13,625
Current assets	49,085	-	-	49,085
Liabilities				
Amounts falling due in one year	(2,700)	-	-	(2,700)
Amounts falling due after one year	(500)	-	-	(500)
	83,240	7,775	2,495	93,510

Part 2

Receipts and Payments Accounting

A.   Introduction to Charity Accounting

In 2008/09 alone people gave £13 billion to charities. Of this incredible resource £0.5 billion was given to the Church of England.

As charities we have a major impact on our society, funding or supporting community work that otherwise, if it would seem to be outside the total responsibility of Government, would not happen! So it is easy to see why Governments are interested in all charities. They want to ensure that money given to charities is spent on the charity's aims and not wasted, so that people will keep giving.

To achieve this aim successive UK Governments have been developing charity law for more than 400 years. They have on charity trustees more and more demands as the persons responsible for the work and finances of the charity. The members of the PCC are charity trustees. The Charities Act (2011) defines charities as organisations that aim to provide 'public benefit' in one or more charitable areas or 'purposes'. It has also reinforced the Charity Commission's legal powers to be able to support and regulate charities.

The Charity Commission created the Charities SORP (Accounting and Reporting by Charities: Statement of Recommended Practice), to give us clear guidelines on what information to keep and what reports to produce to meet our legal obligations. The Church of England has adopted the SORP as its standard basis for annual financial reporting by parishes, so that now we can provide the same information to both the Government (for the general public) and the wider church.

B.   What does this mean for you as a parish?

As PCC members we are the Charity Trustees of the parish. We therefore need to understand what money is coming into the church, how we are spending it and why. In order to give a clear account of how the money has been received and spent, each parish has to produce the reports required by law.

These accounts and reports help us to tell people how their money supports the mission of the Church. They will also help us to show that the money given to us for running the parish or for specific aims such as youth or building work was used for those purposes. As PCC members we are responsible for the money, how it is looked after and for providing clear information about all of the money that belongs to the church.

The first step in providing the correct reports is to decide which kind of annual accounts you need to produce and how these will be externally examined. There are two alternative ways of preparing annual accounts:

Accruals accounts or Receipts and Payments-based accounts?

How do you decide? The basic rule is to calculate the gross income of your parish (that is all income before any payments have been made or costs deducted, but excluding any capital received for endowment). If it is:

- Less than £250,000 a year you can choose to prepare either accruals accounts or the easier Receipts and Payments based accounts.

- Over £250,000 a year you must report using accruals accounts. A separate guide is available for preparing accruals accounts.

If your income is less than £250,000 per year, Receipts and Payments is the easier form of annual accounting for your parish. Unless there are particular reasons why accruals accounts are needed for your parish, new treasurers are advised to choose Receipts and Payments unless they are experienced in accruals accounting.

Accruals accounts are required by law if the PCC's annual gross income is over £250,000.

The following guidance is for Receipts and Payments accounting only.

C.   What are Receipts and Payments accounts?

As the name suggests they are a way of summarising all receipts (the cash coming into the parish, such as Sunday giving, special collections, other gifts of money, etc.) and all payments (the cash going out of the parish, such as electricity, parish share, giving to other good causes, etc.). To give a full picture, they also need to summarise the assets (what you owned) and liabilities (what you owed) at the year end.

All Church of England parishes have a financial year that is the calendar year: **1 January – 31 December.**

The 'Annual Report and Accounts' has four components that you need to provide at the end of the year.

You produce:

1.   Trustees' Annual Report

2.   A Receipts and Payments Account

3.   A Statement of Assets and Liabilities

and an Independent Examiner of your choice will produce the fourth report:

4.   Independent Examiner's Report on the accounts

> If you are not sure what to look for in an Independent Examiner, how to appoint one, what information to give to them or even how to find one, guidance can be found on the Charity Commission website.

The Charity Commission sets the ground rules for the design and content of the Trustees' Annual Report and the Independent Examiner's Report. There is no design that you 'must' follow for the Receipts and Payments Account and the Statement of Assets and Liabilities. You must give at least the minimum information required by law and the wider church. Obviously, it is best to present this in a consistent way from year to year. The examples shown in this booklet give the recommended trustees' report and annual accounts designs from the national Church's perspective, and in the light of Charity Commission recommendations.

This guidance aims to make annual reporting easier. By producing the recommended reports and accounts you will also have provided all the information required by law.

However, before we get into the reports and accounts themselves we need to look at a basic principle of charity accounting – the use of trust funds.

D.   What are Trust Funds and why are they important?

As we said in the introduction, people give money on trust with the expectation that the PCC will use it appropriately. Let's unpack this a little:

The parish must track all of the money it is given to show that the donor's wishes have been met. As that money comes into the parish for so many different things and in so many different ways, how can it be tracked? The answer is by using 'funds'; accounting records that record money according to the specific purposes for which it was given.

This way of looking at money is well known to many householders who, for example, receive a weekly wage and in order to 'make ends meet' then allocate it to various needs or 'funds':

● giving to 'good causes'

● food shopping

● mortgage or rent

● utility bills

● clothes

- holidays

- and the little bit left over!

The weekly wage has come into one household but it has been allocated for various purposes.

Now let's look at how 'funds' work in a parish where the 'wages' are the money **given** to us by people who choose to say what the money they have given is to be spent on. For example, in one week:

The normal Sunday collection is received (**£450**) to keep the parish running, as part of its mission and ministry. It is **unrestricted money for the PCC's general purposes**, to be used in whatever way the PCC decides. As in a household most of the money given to a parish is unrestricted.

The same week a special collection is also taken for youth work (**£250**). This time it is clear that the people who donated it expect their money to be used for youth work. It is **restricted money** (under trust law). Not even the PCC or the vicar can give permission for it to be used on anything else.

The parish is grateful to receive a legacy of **£50,000** for youth work. The will states that this money must be invested, and only the income (interest or dividends) can be spent. This is **endowed money** and it has been **restricted** to the youth work, so it can't be used for anything else.

On Monday morning all of the money, a total of £50,700, goes into the bank, and the parish accounts show:

Bank current account receives: £50,700 from giving, and out of this:

- £450 is allocated to the General Fund (unrestricted money for spending)

- £250 is allocated to the Youth Fund (restricted money for spending)

- £50,000 is allocated to the Youth Endowment Fund (restricted money for investing).

All the money your parish receives can be put in one bank account so long as you have recorded to which fund the money belongs. As you spend money you also need to show which fund has been used, for example: whenever money is used for youth work it should normally come out of the Youth Fund. When the parish electricity bill needs paying it comes out of the General Fund.

Finally, if the PCC decides, for example, to spend more on youth work, it can move money from the General Fund into a Designated fund, in this case the 'Youth Designated Fund'. That money is still unrestricted, so if the roof blows off, the PCC can undesignate the money, and move it back to the General Fund to use for repairing the roof!

For more information on types of trust fund, see Appendix One : 'What are Funds and Fund Types?'

E. What do you have to do to produce your 'Annual Report and Accounts'?

Put simply you need to summarise:

1. What went into the bank, for what fund (purpose) and where it came from (receipts);

2. What came out of the bank, from what fund and what it was spent on (payments);

3. Details of any investments and other assets as at the end of the year (even if sold since) and to what fund they belong;

4. Details of any loans, unpaid bills or other liabilities as at the end of the year (even if paid since) and to what fund they relate.

To do this:

You need to start by thinking about how money is received and spent by the PCC and then deciding on the most sensible account headings to use. It is likely that the parish is already using account headings and they may need little change.

Some basic practical and consistent account headings have been identified for you to adopt or use as a checklist. They relate to parish life and link easily to the Receipts and Payments reports and the Annual Return of Parish Finance report. See Appendix Two.

The following examples use these account headings:

Receipt Account Headings	Payment Account Headings
Planned Giving	Parish Share
Collections at Services	Mission Giving and Donations
Gift Aid recovered	Church Running Expenses
Receipts from church activities (e.g. Fees for weddings and funerals)	Fund Raising Activities (e.g. Costs of fetes and other events)

Example individual account descriptions (column 4) are given in Appendix Two. The individual account descriptions included in each heading can be as detailed as you wish. Each time you get or spend money you also need to record the fund that you used. If you use a cashbook or spreadsheets, you simply add extra columns for the funds. Church specific software will manage this for you.

Using the limited number of categories and account headings shown in Appendix Two enables your accounts to be compared with other parishes. Doing this gives an overall picture of how parishes within each diocese or across the country are getting and spending their money.

The category groupings bring together similar account headings. For example, all donations are shown as Voluntary Receipts and the running costs of the church are shown as Church Activities. The headings given here are suggested for parish use, and are in line with guidance from the Charity Commission and the Return of Parish Finance.

There are two main sections to the accounts: 'Receipts' and 'Payments' and these are divided into categories and account headings to give more detail. Using the examples above, the receipts would be grouped together in categories:

Receipts categories for reporting	Receipt account headings
Voluntary Receipts	Planned Giving
	Collections at Services
	Gift Aid Recovered
Church Activities	Receipts from church activities (e.g. Fees for weddings and funerals)

Using the examples above the Payments would be grouped together in categories:

Payments categories for reporting	Payment accounts headings
Church Activities	Parish Share
	Mission Giving and Donations
	Church Running Expenses
Costs of generating funds	Fund Raising Activities (e.g. Costs of fetes and other events)

For examples of receipt and payment account headings linked to the appropriate categories see **Appendix Two.**

Once the account headings have been decided and the funds that the money belongs to has been identified, you are ready to start recording receipts and payments.

F.   Practical hints and tips

1.   You do not need to record **depreciation**.

2.   **Recording money you receive or pay that covers more than one account heading:**
     For example, You may be given money or make payments that cover more than one account heading such as purchasing Bibles partly for the bookstall and partly as a gift in kind to a missionary society.

     You need to divide the money between the different activity account headings – it is called **apportionment** and should be done on a '**reasonable basis**'. This means that if 20% of the Bibles were for the bookstall and 80% for the mission then 20% of the cost would be shown as Bookstall Costs and 80% as Mission Grants.

3.   **Recording money you receive or pay that covers more than one fund:**
     You may receive or pay out money that relates to more than one fund. For example, building work that is partly normal maintenance and partly special repairs for which an appeal for funds was made and so should come partly out of the General Fund and partly out of the Building Restricted Fund.

     You need to divide the money between the different funds. This is also **apportionment** and should be done on a '**reasonable basis**'. For example, if the building work done is 50% normal maintenance and 50% improvement then the payment will be split half to the General Fund and half to the Building Restricted Fund.

4.   **Netting off is not allowed.** You must show all receipts and payments gross, so for example, if you have a fete which costs £100 for materials/publicity and you raise £500 from the fete, your accounts must not show the receipts less the payments which would be an overall receipt of £400.

     In this case you must show:

     a.   Receipts = £500

     b.   Payments = £100

     However, where money simply passes through the PCC's bank account, but the funds do not belong to the PCC, then neither the receipt nor the payment should be recorded.

5.   **Return of Parish Finance Report:** each parish is asked to complete an annual return of financial information. The information is gathered under certain categories in a similar way to the Receipts and Payments Account.

     There is a standard Return of Parish Finance Report and by relating individual account headings to the relevant category the information can be gathered quite simply. **Appendix Three** shows the example account headings related to the appropriate categories. Some dioceses require additional information, which can be added in a similar way.

G.   What reports do you have to produce?

Once you have reached 31 December and all of your receipts and payments have been recorded (see the end of year checklist) you are ready to produce your 'Annual Accounts'. You need to produce:

     1.   Trustees' Annual Report
     2.   A Receipts and Payments Account
     3.   A Statement of Assets and Liabilities

As it is always helpful to see what these reports would look like in a parish setting we have provided the full Receipts and Payments reports for a fictional Church of England parish called St Emilions. We will explain what each report needs to include (and why) and you can see this in the St Emilions example.

1. Trustees' Annual Report (TAR)

This report gives you the chance to tell everyone the aims of the church and what you are doing to make them happen. You can share 'good news' stories and how people's giving made them possible.

Trustees are collectively responsible for this report, and the drafting should not just be left to the treasurer. Its function is to give a clear and concise description of the mission and ministry of the church and how it is governed, on the year's activities and achievements and plans for the future and on the adequacy of it's funds. Also remember that this report is meant for everyone so that even strangers can feel they understand why and how the church works.

What is in the Trustees' Annual Report?

The following pages review the report section by section, with a brief guidance note, followed by the example.

2010 Report and Accounts for the Parochial Church Council of St Emilion's Church, Barchester

Aims and purposes

Information required	What you need to include
Aims and purposes	Every Church of England church has the same aim: 'To promote the whole mission of the Church, pastoral, evangelistic, social and ecumenical'. You will need to show any buildings etc. that the PCC is responsible for in the local situation.

St Emilion's Parochial Church Council (PCC) has the responsibility of cooperating with the incumbent, the Reverend Samuel Weller, in promoting in the ecclesiastical parish, the whole mission of the Church, pastoral, evangelistic, social and ecumenical. The PCC is also specifically responsible for the maintenance of the Church Centre complex of St Emilion's, The Green, Barchester.

Objectives and activities

Information required	What you need to include
Objectives and Activities	How you are trying to fulfil the aims of the church for the benefit of everyone in the church and community. For example the PCC may have become aware that there are no daytime activities for families with small children and decided to try to meet their needs – this would be fulfilling pastoral and social aims.

The PCC is committed to enabling as many people as possible to worship at our church and to become part of our parish community at St Emilion. The PCC maintains an overview of worship throughout the parish and makes suggestions on how our services can involve the many groups that live within our parish. Our services and worship put faith into practice through prayer and scripture, music and sacrament.

When planning our activities for the year, we have considered the Commission's guidance on public benefit and, in particular, the supplementary guidance on charities for the advancement of religion. In particular, we try to enable ordinary people to live out their faith as part of our parish community through:

● Worship and prayer; learning about the gospel; and developing their knowledge and trust in Jesus;

● Provision of pastoral care for people living in the parish;

● Missionary and outreach work.

To facilitate this work it is important that we maintain the fabric of the Church of St Emilion and the Church Centre Complex.

Achievements and performance

Information required	What you need to include
Aims and purposes	Every Church of England church has the same aim: 'To promote the whole mission of the Church, pastoral, evangelistic, social and ecumenical'. You will need to show any buildings etc. that the PCC is responsible for in the local situation.

Worship and prayer

The PCC is keen to offer a range of services during the week and over the course of the year that our community find both beneficial and spiritually fulfilling. For example, evening prayers provide a quiet, intimate and reflective environment for worship while opportunities are provided for people to engage in more outgoing worship such as that provided by the youth group within our parish.

This year we have been successful in welcoming more families into our church and have agreed a new style of Family Worship on the morning of the 3rd Sunday each month. This has meant that special arrangements have had to be made for baptisms and for welcoming the families at corporate worship on the 1st Sunday of each month. It is pleasing to be able to report that the new arrangements have been well received since they came into operation during September. They will be reviewed by the PCC after 12 months. In addition, a great deal of time and thought was spent during the year on making best use of the new services. Many have said how much easier it is to follow the services now that they are printed out in booklets.

All are welcome to attend our regular services. At present there are 173 parishioners on the Church Electoral Roll, 91 of whom are not resident within the parish. 18 names were added during the year and 9 were removed either through death or because they moved away from the parish. The average weekly attendance, counted during October, was 107, but this number increased at festivals and two Christmas carol services had to be held to seat all those who wished to attend.

As well as our regular services, we enable our community to celebrate and thank God at the milestones of the journey through life. Through baptism we thank God for the gift of life, in marriage public vows are exchanged with God's blessing and through funeral services friends and family express their grief and give thanks for the life which is now complete in this world and to commend the person into God's keeping. We have celebrated 25 baptisms and 15 weddings and held 26 funerals in our church this year.

Deanery Synod

Three members of the PCC sit on the deanery synod. This provides the PCC with an important link between the parish and the wider structures of the church. This year the PCC has also focused its attention on the questions posed to parishes in the deanery about the most effective deployment of stipendiary and non-stipendiary clergy.

The Church Centre Complex

We want our church to be open to our community for private prayer. Unfortunately, since the theft of valuable church artefacts from St Augustus Church, in the neighbouring parish, we have felt unable to leave the church open at all times for private worship. We are however pleased that a rota of parishioners has enabled us to open the church at weekends and for all public holidays in the past year.

The state of the nave roof has been causing concern for some time. After many years, during which routine maintenance has been carried out, a detailed report on its condition will be prepared by the architect at the next routine inspection in April 2011. We have already anticipated the need for major structural renewal, and it is our policy to make provisions from general income in the hope that an urgent appeal can be avoided.

The kitchen in the Church Hall was refurbished during August and the new environment meets the stringent health and safety requirements and allows us to continue the old people's luncheon club on Saturdays. 18 people regularly attend at our luncheon club, 12 of whom are parishioners. We were particularly pleased to be able to extend the services of our club to the members of the Barchester Green Methodist Chapel luncheon club when the death of Alice Luther, the main organiser of that club forced its closure.

During the week the hall is used by our mothers and toddlers group on Wednesdays. Fifteen children and their carers have been regular attenders at the mothers and toddlers group. During the summer the group organised two outings including older siblings during the school holidays. In July, 20 children and their parents went for the day to Longleat and later in the holidays we had the hottest day of the year for our family outing to New Milton.

The crèche runs in the hall on Tuesday and Thursday mornings. There are 12 regular attenders at the crèche which is organised by Sally Pincent, the council's peripatetic childcare coordinator who runs crèches at our church as well as at St Augustus on Mondays and Wednesdays. She has a rota of volunteers from the parish who help her, all of whom have been CRB checked. The crèche had an OFSTED inspection during the year and passed with flying colours.

Pastoral care

Some members of our parish are unable to attend church due to sickness or age. Reverend Samuel Weller has visited all church members who have requested it, to celebrate communion with them either at their homes or in hospital. Miss Finching has continued to organise a rota of volunteers to visit all who are sick or unable to get out for any other reason to keep them in touch with church life.

Mission and evangelism

Helping those in need is a demonstration of our faith. The Mission and Evangelism Committee is to be congratulated on its fund-raising efforts. £1,350 was raised for the Southern Africa Famine appeal. It is good that these efforts on behalf of others can be combined with opportunities for fellowship.

Our parish magazine is distributed quarterly to all parishioners on the Church Electoral Roll and available at the Church Hall. The magazine keeps our parishioners informed of the important matters affecting our church and articles that help develop our knowledge and trust in Jesus.

Ecumenical relationships

The church is a member of Churches Together in Barchester and of the Salisbury Interfaith Forum. We have held joint services on the fourth Sunday of every month with the Barchester Green Methodist Church and for the first time this year have joined with them both for our Lent courses and to run an Alpha course in the autumn. The Alpha course has led a number of people to attend other church activities and services. We have also worked with Barchester Green Methodist Church and Millfield Baptist Church to deliver a flyer to every home in the town advertising the Christmas services of all three churches.

Financial review

Information required	What you need to include
Financial Review	A brief explanation of how the money has come in and been spent. Explaining what has happened to the money straight after talking about the church's achievements helps people to see the links especially if you describe how giving was used. You also need to explain the 'Reserves Policy', the amount of money that the church is keeping for a 'rainy day' or future projects. The Charity Commission understands the need for some reserves but the church has to remember that the money was given to do the work of the church and not just sit in a bank!

Total receipts on unrestricted funds were £64,200 of which £42,000 was unrestricted voluntary donations, and a further £8,700 was from Gift Aid. Restricted donations of £5,800 were also received and are detailed in the Financial Statements. The freehold house at 36 Church Road continues to be let temporarily, which provided a gross income of £3,700.

The planned giving through envelopes and banker's orders increased by 8% and it was good to see the use of Gift Aid envelopes increased. Total income, including tax recovered but excluding the legacy, went up by only 3% compared with last year. This was partly due to the Christmas Bazaar not being held this year. We were grateful for a pecuniary legacy of £1,000 from the estate of Mrs Mary Rudge. £2,000 was set aside towards the cost of the much-needed cleaning of the organ. The work was completed in time for Christmas.

£61,350 was spent from unrestricted funds to provide the Christian ministry from St Emilion's Church, including the contribution to the diocesan parish share that increased by 12% in the year and largely provides the stipends and housing for the clergy.

The sum that the churches in the deanery have to find is shared between the churches according to a formula that is based mainly on a head count of the congregations. We have to find more of the sum at St Emilion's as the size of our congregation increased more compared with other churches.

The net result for the year was an excess of receipts over payments of £2,850 on unrestricted funds. Adding bank and deposit balances brought forward at the beginning of the year, the balances carried forward at 31 December on unrestricted funds totalled £10,450 of which £5,300 has been set aside to meet the costs of cleaning and maintaining the church organ and is carried forward as a designated fund.

Reserves policy

Information required	What you need to include
Reserves Policy	In this section the PCC needs to summarise its Reserves Policy, and to report where its reserves stand in relation to this policy, and action that the PCC will take to address any imbalance. In addition to cash balances, amounts payable to and by the PCC at the year end should also be included (e.g. Gift Aid claim made but not yet received, and bills received but not yet paid.)

It is PCC policy to try to maintain a balance on unrestricted funds which equates to at least three months' unrestricted payments. This is equivalent to £15,000. It is held to smooth out fluctuations in cash flow and to meet emergencies. The cash balance of £10,450 held on unrestricted (including designated) funds at the year end, together with the amounts payable to and by the PCC, was less than half of this target. It is the PCC's hope to increase this over time, as and when investment income recovers.

The balance of £17,050 in the Fabric restricted fund is retained towards meeting the cost of the nave roof repairs detailed above. It is our policy to invest £5,000 of our fund balances with the CCLA Church of England Deposit Fund, and the remainder in the CCLA Church of England Investment Fund.

Optional information

Information required	What you need to include
Optional Information	This section can be used to thank people for example the volunteers and perhaps to give a special mention to someone for their work.

Volunteers

We would like to thank all the volunteers who work so hard to make our church the lively and vibrant community it is. In particular we want to mention our churchwardens Mrs Allen and Mr Tapley who have worked so tirelessly on our behalf and Mrs Neckett who has helped us all to understand the church's accounts and its finances.

Structure, governance and management

Information required	What you need to include
Structure, Governance and Management	This is the information that we think we all know but not everyone does! The question is how is the church organised and who decides what? This is where you explain what the PCC is and how it is elected, its responsibilities, and any sub-committees that have been set up. It needs to include a brief note on any significant transactions with PCC members or closely related persons.

The method of appointment of PCC members is set out in the Church Representation Rules. At St Emilion's the membership of the PCC consists of the incumbent (our vicar), churchwardens, the reader and members elected by those members of the congregation who are on the electoral roll of the church. All those who congregation are encouraged to register on the Electoral Roll and stand for election to the PCC.

The PCC members are responsible for making decisions on all matters of general concern and importance to the parish including deciding on how the funds of the PCC are to be spent. New members receive initial training into the workings of the PCC.

The full PCC met six times during the year with an average level of attendance of 80%. Given its wide responsibilities the PCC has a number of committees each dealing with a particular aspect of parish life.

These committees, which include worship, mission and outreach and fabric and finance, are all responsible to the PCC and report back to it regularly with minutes of their decisions being received by the full PCC and discussed as necessary.

Administrative Information

Information required	What you need to include
Administration	As the name suggests this is the basic information on the church: ● The address of the church ● Contact details ● The legal standing of the PCC ● PCC membership for the year of this report (ex-officio, elected or co-opted)

St Emilion's Church is situated in The Green, Barchester. It is part of the Diocese of Salisbury within the Church of England. The correspondence address is The Vicarage, Church Street, Barchester. The PCC is a body corporate (PCC Powers Measure 1956, Church Representation Rules 2006) and a charity currently excepted from registration with the Charity Commission.

PCC members who have served at any time from 1 January 2010 until the date this report was approved are:

Ex Officio members:

- Incumbent: The Reverend Samuel Weller (Chairman)

- Reader: Mr Robert Sawyer

- Wardens: Mrs Arabella Allen

Mr Mark Tapley Vice chairman

Elected members:

- Mr Frederick Trent representative on Deanery Synod

- Mr Peter Magnus Secretary, representative on Deanery Synod

- Mr John Fielding representative on Deanery Synod

- Miss Flora Finching (From 5 April 2010)

- Mrs Charlotte Neckett Treasurer

- Mr George Radfoot

- Miss Edith Granger

- Mrs Tilly Slowboy

- Miss Emily Wardle (Until 5 April 2010)

- Mr Mark Walker

- Miss Emma Haredale

- Mr Julius Handford (Until 5 April 2010)

- Miss Elizabeth Hexham

- Mr Ralph Nickleby (From 5 April 2010)

Approved by the PCC on 8 March 2011 and signed on their behalf by the Reverend Samuel Weller (PCC chairman)

2. Receipts and Payments account

The first financial report shows how the parish's cash was received and spent and how this related to your funds. You can produce a receipt and payment summary for:

1. each fund – summarising all of the cash going in to or out of each fund separately;

2. each type of fund – summarising all of the cash going in to or out of each fund type separately; or

3. all three types of fund combined in a single statement with each type in a separate column.

The recommended option is **option 3**. However, certain information is needed to complete the Receipts and Payments Summary. The following table shows you the questions you need to answer and where the information is put on the report.

Section on the Account	What question is being asked by the section
Receipts	What cash did you receive? This will include under 'Other receipts' the money you got (if any) from selling any asset, (such as a building or land) or investments.
Payments	What cash did you spend – and on what? This will include under 'Other payments' any money you converted into other valuable assets (such as buying a building or land) or investments.
Excess of receipts (or payments)	Were your receipts more or less than your payments? In other words did the PCC's cash assets increase or decrease?
Transfers	How much money did you move between different funds?
Bank balance at beginning of year	How much was in the bank when you started the year?
Bank balance at end of year	How much was in the bank when you ended the year?
Last year's totals for comparison (Although this is not legally required, it is strongly recommended to help the reader better understand the accounts.)	Was this year better or worse than last year and in what way?
All amounts should to be rounded to the nearest £.	**Remember there is no netting off. Expenses and costs must be shown in full.**

In the St Emilions report and accounts you can see how this works in practice:

PAROCHIAL CHURCH COUNCIL OF ST EMILION'S CHURCH, BARCHESTER

Financial Statements for the Year Ended 31 December 2012

Receipts and Payments Accounts

	Note	Unrestricted Fund	Unrestricted Designated Fund	Restricted Fund	Endowment Fund	Total 2012	Total 2011
		£	£	£	£	£	£
Receipts							
Voluntary receipts:							
Planned giving		29,400	-	-	-	29,400	27,200
Collections at services		9,900	-	-	-	9,900	10,600
All other giving/voluntary receipts	5a	2,700	-	5,800	-	8,500	7,050
Gift Aid recovered		8,700	-	-	-	8,700	8,300
		50,700	-	5,800	-	56,500	53,150
Activities for generating funds	5b	3,500	-	-	-	3,500	4,250
Investment income	5c	4,600	-	950	-	5,550	5,300
Church activities	5d	5,400	-	-	-	5,400	5,150
Other receipts*		-	-	-	-	-	-
Total receipts		64,200	-	6,750	-	70,950	67,850
Payments							
Church activities:							
Parish share		41,500	-	-	-	41,500	37,050
Clergy and Staffing costs		1,900	-	-	-	1,900	1,800
Church running expenses	5e	13,700	-	1,750	-	15,450	15,250
Hall running costs		1,200	-	-	-	1,200	1,200
Mission giving and donations	5f	2,550	-	1,350	-	3,900	2,550
		60,850	-	3,100	-	63,950	57,850
Cost of generating funds		500	-	-	-	500	500
Governance Costs*		-	-	-	-	-	-
Other Payments*		-	-	-	-	-	-
Total payments		61,350	-	3,100	-	64,450	58,350
Excess of receipts over payments		2,850	-	3,650	-	6,500	9,500
Transfers between funds	4	(2,000)	2,000	-	-	-	-
		850	2,000	3,650	-	6,500	9,500
Cash at bank and in hand at 1 Jan		4,300	3,300	13,400	-	21,000	11,500
Cash at bank and in hand at 31 Dec		5,150	5,300	17,050	-	27,500	21,000

*Note that where there are no amounts to be entered for either of the two years, these headings need not be included. (e.g. Other Receipts, Governance Costs, Other Payments). Categories and account headings within them can be added or removed in the order shown in Appendix Two as needed. (e.g. Church Activities)

3. Statement of assets and liabilities

This report shows the total financial resources of the parish and how they are allocated to funds. The following table shows what information to include in each section:

Statement of Assets and Liabilities	
Section of the Statement	**What question is being asked by the section:**
Cash	**How much money is in the bank / petty cash accounts at the end of the year?** The amount shown on the Receipts and Payments Account
Other monetary assets	**What other money do you have or is owed to you?** This includes such items as: ● Gift Aid claimed but not yet received ● Loans made by the parish ● Money owed for services or work provided by the parish ● Legacies where entitlement is proved, but the money (or other asset) has not yet been received.
Investments assets	**What investments do you have?** This includes investments and property or land that brings income to the parish or increases in value. The amount shown is either the deposit balance or the amount paid for the investment.
Assets retained for Church use.	**What other assets of this kind do you have e.g. land, houses?** If you don't know the cost, you can just describe these assets and how long they have been in the ownership of the PCC. You don't have to value them nor show an estimated or insurance value.
Liabilities	**What amounts did you owe at the end of the year?** This includes such items as: ● Amount of any loans to the PCC still to be paid back ● Payroll deductions and employer contributions relating to the financial year that are unpaid at the end of the year ● Only money actually owed at the year-end (or the best estimate of it) should be included
	All amounts should to be rounded to the nearest £.

You can see how the Statement of Assets and Liabilities might look in practice in the St Emilions example:

Statement of Assets and Liabilities

	Note	Unrestricted Fund (£)	Unrestricted Designated Fund (£)	Restricted Fund (£)	Endowment Fund (£)	Total 2012 (£)	Total 2011 (£)
Cash Funds							
Bank Current Account		400	–	–	–	400	350
Deposit Account		4,750	5,300	17,050	–	27,100	20,650
		5,150	5,300	17,050	–	27,500	21,000
Other Monetary Assets							
Income Tax recoverable		2,240	–	–	–	2,240	–
Investment Assets							
Investment Fund Shares at market value	3	–	–	–	20,000	20,000	19,500
Assets retained for Church use	2	59,000	–	–	–	59,000	59,000
Liabilities – organ clean/tune		–	6,200	–	–	6,200	–

When you are deciding what needs to be shown as an asset or liability you need to ask yourself is it vital information? This means if you left that information out would it make the financial position harder to understand?

For example, at the end of the year you owe a builder £5.00 for wood – this amount will not make a big difference to the church so need not be shown. Your Independent Examiner can give you advice if you are not sure.

Although you are putting a lot of information into these accounts there are often things that you want to explain or add. For example you may need to explain what your funds are given for or any transfers between funds that you made. Or where you don't know the end of year open market value of an asset that isn't a sum of money (e.g. a lease on a building; stocks and shares; a bequest of such assets) you can just give identifying information about the asset, it's condition and use, also its cost (if purchased). You can do all this by adding 'notes' to your accounts.

Notes to the accounts may help the reader to understand the accounts better. For example, you might choose to include further details about payments and receipts e.g. a breakdown of church running costs. There is a balance to be struck between providing useful additional information to the reader, and providing so much detail that it can confuse rather than help. These notes can be written as part of your Statement of Assets and Liabilities or else within the Trustees Annual Report. You can see how this works in practice in the St Emilions reports.

4.   Independent Examiner's Report

Who checks our accounts?

As a parish you need to show that your accounts comply with the Charities Act. To do this you have chosen to publish Receipt and Payment accounts summarised from what you have recorded as the cash going into and out of the parish during the year.

At the end of the year you must have the accounts checked by an independent person who is not on the PCC (or any PCC sub-committee) and who understands charity accounting (this applies to all PCCs under Church Regulations). Your Independent Examiner will need to examine the accounts and underlying records within the context of the Annual Report, and provide you with a statutory form of Report on the accounts.

For guidance on recruiting an Independent Examiner, see p. 58.

H.   What happens next?

The PCC then needs to approve the Trustees' Annual Report, with the accounts and Independent Examiner's Report attached. Note, the accounts are the responsibility of the whole PCC and not just the treasurer. Then the Report and Accounts are ready for a wider audience.

Who do you give the Report and Accounts to?

The accounts are published – put on notice boards within the church at least seven days before the Annual Parochial Church Meeting. As PCC treasurer, you will normally be required to explain the accounts to the Annual Parochial Church Meeting. Copies of these reports are sent to the Diocesan Office with the Parish Return of Finance report.

The accounts are public documents so every member of the public has a right to see them and can request a copy!

I.   End of year checklists

Before sending your accounts to the Independent Examiner have you:

Question	Answer
Ensured that you have included all bank accounts and funds relevant to the PCC?	The Receipts and Payments Account(s) must include all receipts and payments that the PCC is responsible for. Examples might include youth funds, flower funds, coffee money, lunch clubs etc. that have separate bank or cash accounts.
Properly recorded all loose plate giving?	Normal Sunday collections have been recorded as part of the General Fund. Collections made for special purposes have been recorded against the relevant fund(s).
Recorded any money paid out as cash from Sunday collections?	All money collected should normally be banked gross. If a small payment has been made out of cash, this should be recorded as a Petty Cash receipt and then as a Petty Cash payment, with evidence of what the money was used for – shop receipt etc. (The relevant fund(s) must be recorded in each case.)
Recorded all Standing Orders?	Only Standing Orders that have been paid or received within the financial year should be recorded in that year.
Kept all Gift Aid records up to date?	This may be managed by a Gift Aid Secretary.
Recorded the tax reclaimed on Gift Aid?	Any Gift Aid received on money for a specific fund must be allocated to that fund. You may have sent your gift aid claim to the HMRC before the end of the year, but you will only record the gift aid you have received in the bank during the year. The Statement of Assets and Liabilities will record any significant sums of Gift Aid claimed from HMRC, but not yet received.
Properly recorded endowment fund interest?	This has been recorded as income against the restricted fund the endowment relates to or to the General Fund if there were no restrictions. It should not be recorded as income to the endowment funds.
Ensured all payments are properly evidenced?	Are all payments supported by receipts, invoices, expense claims, or other paperwork?
Ensured any new designation of funds made by the PCC during the year have been recorded?	If the PCC has decided to designate any of its unrestricted funds during the year, this needs to be recorded.

What are Funds and Fund Types?

Funds are the way in which Charity law requires you to track money given by your donors or received from other sources. Why is the Government interested in this? They want people to be confident that the money they give for good causes is not misused or wasted but properly used. And, hopefully, people will then continue to give!

People give to the church for all sorts of reasons. To help track the money, it is allocated to a fund. To help you know how to use the money in any particular fund, it is also allocated to a 'fund type'. Most of the money a PCC receives will be for spending on the PCC's normal activities. This money is 'Unrestricted Income'. Sometimes the giver will specify the activities that they wish the money to be used for. This money is 'Restricted Income'. Occasionally money may be given for the PCC to retain rather than spend on activities. This money is 'Endowment Capital'.

If you have unrestricted funds which the PCC want to use for a particular purpose, the chosen amount can be earmarked as an unrestricted 'Designated Fund' for that particular purpose. Each time you receive or spend money you need to say which fund it is for. The following table shows what each type of fund is and how it can be used:

The Fund type	Where the money comes from	How it can be used	Where it can be banked	Who decides how the money is used.
Unrestricted Income: The General Fund	Normal Sunday or other collections with no special purpose Gifts for the Parish Gift Days for the general work of the parish Grants for the general work of the parish Money given for use at the vicar or PCC's discretion	For the upkeep of the parish For purposes agreed by the PCC For the Parish Share For giving to other appeals or charities	In any bank or deposit account so long as it has been recorded as allocated to the General Fund	The PCC
Unrestricted Designated Funds It remains unrestricted money but is allocated for a particular purpose.	It is money given to the General Fund that the PCC has allocated for a particular purpose	Only for the purpose decided by the PCC	In any bank or deposit account so long as it has been recorded as allocated to a designated fund	The PCC

Restricted Income: Funds given to the PCC to be spent for a specific purpose	Special collections, gifts and donations, appeals, Gift Days or legacies where the PCC or the Donor has indicated that the money will be used for a specific purpose	Only for the purpose for which it was given	In any bank or deposit account so long as it has been recorded as allocated to the correct restricted fund	The Donor or terms of the Appeal (or in certain situations the Charity Commission), or the PCC with Charity Commission consent
Endowment Capital: Funds given to the PCC for longer-term retention rather than immediate spending They are capital funds, but can be unrestricted or restricted purposes as specified by the donor	Legacies, capital gifts, capital grants, capital appeals	Only for the benefit of the PCC, and restricted to any special purpose for which it was given	In any deposit or investment account so long as it has been recorded as allocated to the general or specific endowment fund as appropriate	The Donor or terms of the Appeal (if the donor has not indicated that they can only be used for something specific, then the PCC decides)

Hints and tips

Where possible, use restricted money first. For example, if you have a Youth Restricted fund and the bill you are paying is for a youth event it is likely that you can use this fund.

Why is this important? Restricted money can only be used for the purpose for which it was first given. Using restricted money when you can will leave more money in your General Fund. This will give you the greatest flexibility to meet whatever happens later in the year!

When having a Gift Day or appeal if possible make it for the general work of the church – this will give you the most flexibility when using the money.

If you have a specific Appeal or Gift Day make it clear that any extra money will be put into the General Fund. For example, if you have an appeal for the roof which is so successful that the roof is repaired with £500 left over, unless you have told people that any extra money will go to the General Fund this £500 must remain in the Roof Restricted Fund.

Telling people what you will do if you get too much money (or if so little money that the project has to be aborted) means that they are fully aware of how their money will be used and so have the choice. It will also avoid having restricted money, which you cannot use.

When you claim Gift Aid on donations it must go to the fund to which the original money was given. This means that if a person gives you money for the youth work in the church it is restricted to youth work and so is any Gift Aid you claim on that money.

Receipt and Payment Account Categories and Headings

The following tables show how each account heading fits into the correct Receipt or Payment category.
The table is based on, but not identical to, the Annual Return of Parish Finance Categories at Appendix Three.

Receipt or Payment	Category	Account Heading	Account Description	APR Note #
Receipts	Voluntary Receipts	Planned giving	Gift Aid – Bank	01
			Gift Aid – Envelopes	01
			Other planned giving	02
		Collections at Services	Loose plate collections	03
			Special collections	03
		All other giving / voluntary receipts	Gift Days	04
			Giving through church boxes	04
			Donations appeals etc.	05
			Cash received from Legacies	07
			Recurring grants	08
			Non-recurring one-off grants	08A
		Gift Aid recovered	Gift Aid recovered	06
	Activities for generating funds	Fund-raising	Church fetes etc.	09
			Parish Magazine – advertising	12
	Investment Income	Income from Investments	Dividends	10
			Bank and building society interest	10
			Rent from lands or buildings owned by the PCC.	10
	Church Activities	Receipts from church activities	Fees for weddings and funerals	11
			Bookstall and magazine sales	12
			Church hall lettings – objects related	12
	Other Receipts	Other receipts	Insurance claims	13
			Sales of fixed assets	13
			Other funds generated e.g sale of investments	13
Payments	Church Activities	Parish Share	Parish share	19
		Clergy and Staffing	Salaries and wages of parish staff	20
			National Insurance of parish staff	20
			Pension Contributions of parish staff	20
			Working expenses of clergy	21
			Council tax	21
			Parsonage house expenses	21
			Water rates – vicarage	21
			Clergy telephone	21
			Visiting speakers / locums	23
		Church Running Expenses	Education	21/22
			Parish training and mission	22
			Church running – insurance	23
			Church office – telephone	23

Church of England Annual Return of Parish Finance Receipts and Payments Categories

Receipts Categories

Main Category	Which includes	More information on what to include APR	Note #
Voluntary receipts	Tax-efficient planned giving	Money that is given regularly under Gift Aid through a standing order, by envelope scheme, or by cheque. Figures should be net, i.e. receipts planned giving excluding any tax recovered. Also include money given through charity vouchers (gross amount) e.g. CAF or Sovereign Giving and money given through Payroll Giving (gross amount).	01
	Other planned Giving	Money given regularly without Gift Aid through standing order, by envelope scheme, or by cheque.	02
	Collections at Services (On the APR this only refers to loose cash collections at service)	Collections at Sunday, midweek, wedding, baptism and funeral services, and Sunday schools. Include one-off gifts given in collections at services through Gift Aid envelopes (net amount), but exclude money given through planned giving envelopes. Do NOT include collections that go directly to a charity and do not 'go through the PCC books' e.g. Christian Aid Week. Other collections for a specific charity are restricted income Proceeds of annual	03
	Other Recurring Giving /Donations	Gift Days, money given in church boxes and wall safes, and other ad-hoc donations from individuals which are likely to recur in future years.	04
	Non-recurring Giving/Donations	Include one-off donations given outside services. Include the proceeds of all special appeals (which are usually restricted), but also one-off Gift Days for general funds. Include gifts of shares at market value.	05
	Tax recovered through Gift Aid	The amount of tax recovered from HMRC on all money given to the PCC under Gift Aid. This should be split between Gift Aid recovered on restricted and unrestricted donations and allocated to the appropriate fund.	06
	Legacies Received	The capital amount of a legacy, together with interest from the probate process process, should be recorded in the year(s) that it appears in the accounts. (Note that the legacy may have been included as an asset in last year's Statement of Assets and Liabilities.) Any interest from legacy investments should be recorded as income from investments	07
	Income from Grants	External grants received from trusts and other funding bodies for the PCC's general fund or for a restricted purpose. Include VAT recovered through the Listed Places of Worship scheme. This does not include transfers within a benefice.	08
Activities for generating funds	Fund Raising	Money raised from sponsored activities, jumble sales, fetes, and other activities where the primary purpose is fund-raising. Income should be stated gross, and any costs must be recorded separately as payments.	09
Income from investments	Dividends, interest and income from property:	Bank and other deposit interest including any reclaimed tax on investment income. Include dividends from shareholdings. Include rent received from land or buildings owned by PCC.	10
Church activities	Statutory Fees retained by PCC	PCC Fees for weddings, funerals etc. Do not include fees due to the clergy and organist etc. as these are not PCC funds.	11
	Bookstall, hall lettings, magazine sales etc.	Income received by the PCC from trading activities including bookstall, letting of the church hall, sales and advertising of church magazines. Income received from other church activities which are not fundraising	12

activities eg membership fees for groups, payments for events etc.
All trading receipts must be stated as gross figures. The costs must be
recorded separately as payments.

Other receipts	All other receipts	These are often 'capital' in nature: sale of buildings, investments, insurance claims, transfers from term deposits, loans received, repayment of loans made by the church to others; but will also include contributions from other churches in the benefice to shared costs.	13

Payments Categories

Main Category	Which includes	More information on what to include	APR Note #
Costs of generating income	Fund-raising activities	Include the costs of fundraising events, which have contributed to the income recorded in Fund-raising income box above. Also include fees paid to a professional fund-raiser, the costs of a Christian Stewardship campaign and the costs of supporting regular giving e.g. envelopes.	17
Church Activities	Mission Giving and Donations	Include donations to external missions and charities that come from the PCC's receipts. Collections that go directly to external charities should not be included.	18
	Diocesan parish share	All payments made during the year, whether for current, or previous years Share.	19
	Salaries, wages and honoraria	All payments to assistant staff, youth worker, verger, administrator, sexton, organist and choir. Include NI/Pension costs where applicable.	20
	Clergy and staff expenses	Working expenses of the incumbent: e.g. telephone, postage, stationery, travel costs (car and/or public transport), secretarial assistance, office equipment, maintenance of robes, hospitality. Assistant staff: Include costs, as for the incumbent, that are associated with expenses incurred by assistant clergy, pastoral staff and youth workers. Housing: all costs relating to clergy/staff housing paid by the PCC. (including where applicable repair costs, water rates, council tax, and redecoration).	21
	Church Expenses	Mission and Evangelism: cost of outreach, courses, excluding staff salaries	22
		Routine repairs and maintenance.	23
		Insurance	
		Miscellaneous: cleaning materials etc church /office phone.	
		Churchyards all costs involved in their maintenance.	
		Upkeep of services: organ tuning, worship materials, choir robes etc.	
		Church utility bills: total costs of electricity, gas, oil, water etc.	24
		Costs of trading – include the costs associated with the receipts for bookstall, hall lettings, magazine income etc.	25
		Major church repairs: incl repairs that are not routine and internal and external decoration.	27
		Major repairs to other PCC property: incl repairs that are not routine and internal and external decoration.	28
		New building work: new buildings, major alterations and extensions to church or other PCC property and including all associated professional fees and expenses	29
Governance costs	Governance	Costs relating to the governance of the PCC, including any fees for audit or Independent Examination, training of PCC members in their role of Trustees, the production of the annual report, hire charges for any PCC meetings etc.	26
Other payments (incl purchase of FA and investments)	All other payments	All other payments not included above but mainly of a 'capital' nature: Purchase of fixed assets for church purpose. Purchase of investments. Transfers to term deposits. Loans made and repayments of loans etc.	

Part 3

Extracts from Legislation
(inc. Church Accounting Regulations)

The following are extracts from legislation that are referred to above in this publication.

Church Accounting Regulations 2006

Made (Approved by the General Synod)	July 2006
Coming into force	1 August 2006

In pursuance of the power conferred by rule 54(8) of the Church Representation Rules the following Regulations are hereby prescribed by the Business Committee of the General Synod:

Definitions

1. In these Regulations:

    'the Act' means the Charities Act 1993;

    'the Charity Commission' means the Charity Commissioners for England and Wales;

    'Council' means the parochial church council of a parish; and

    'the SORP' means the Statement of Recommended Practice for accounting and reporting by charities published by the Charity Commission on the 4 March 2005 as from time to time amended, and any replacement Statement of Recommended Practice for accounting and reporting by charities published by the Charity Commission.

Revocation of the Church Accounting Regulations 1997 to 2001

2. The Church Accounting Regulations 1997 to 2001 shall continue to have effect in relation to accounts and annual reports of a Council for financial years ending on or before 31 December 2005 but, subject thereto, are hereby revoked.

Requirements in relation to accounts, audit etc.

3. Subject to Regulation 4, a Council shall comply with its obligations under the Act (including any regulations made thereunder) and under the SORP with regard to:

    (a) the keeping of accounting records for the Council;

    (b) the preparation and preservation of annual statements of account for the Council;

    (c) the auditing or independent examination of the statements of account of the Council;

    (d) the transmission of the statements of account of the Council to the Charity Commission;

    (e) the preparation of an annual report for the Council and its transmission to the Charity Commission; and

    (f) the preparation of an annual return for the Council and its transmission to the Charity Commission.

4. If, in respect of a financial year of the Council, the accounts of the Council are not otherwise required by the Act to be audited or examined by an independent examiner, the accounts of the Council for that year shall be examined by an independent examiner; and such examination shall be conducted, and treated for all purposes, as if it were an examination required by the Act.

Commencement and citation

5. (1) These Regulations shall come into force on the 1 August 2006 so as to have effect in relation to accounts and annual reports of a Council for financial years ending on or after 31 December 2006.

    (2) These Regulations may be cited as the Church Accounting Regulations 2006.

Parochial Church Councils (Powers) Measure 1956

1 Definitions

In this Measure:

'Council' means a parochial church council;

'Diocesan Authority' means the Diocesan Board of Finance or any existing or future body appointed by the Diocesan Synod to act as trustees of diocesan trust property;

'Minister' and 'Parish' have the meanings respectively assigned to them in the Rules for the Representation of the Laity.

2 General functions of council

(1) It shall be the duty of the minister and the parochial church council to consult together on matters of general concern and importance to the parish.

(2) The functions of parochial church councils shall include:

(a) cooperation with the minister in promoting in the parish the whole mission of the Church, pastoral, evangelistic, social and ecumenical;

(b) the consideration and discussions of matters concerning the Church of England or any other matters of religious or public interest, but not the declaration of the doctrine of the Church on any question;

(c) making known and putting into effect any provision made by the diocesan synod or the deanery synod, but without prejudice to the powers of the council on any particular matter;

(d) giving advice to the diocesan synod and the deanery synod on any matter referred to the council;

(e) raising such matters as the council consider appropriate with the diocesan synod or deanery synod.

(3) In the exercise of its functions the parochial church council shall take into consideration any expression of opinion by any parochial church meeting.

3 Council to be body corporate

Every council shall be a body corporate by the name of the parochial church council of the parish for which it is appointed and shall have perpetual succession. Any act of the council may be signified by an instrument executed pursuant to a resolution of the council and under the hands or if an instrument under seal is required under the hands and seals of the chairman presiding and two other members of the council present at the meeting at which such resolution is passed.

4 Miscellaneous powers of council

The council of every parish shall have the following powers in addition to any powers conferred by the Constitution or otherwise by this Measure:–

(i) power to frame an annual budget of moneys required for the maintenance of the work of the Church in the parish and otherwise and to take such steps as they think necessary for the raising collecting and allocating of such moneys;

(ii) power to make levy and collect a voluntary church rate for any purpose connected with the affairs of the church including the administrative expenses of the council and the costs of any legal proceedings;

(iii) power jointly with the minister to appoint and dismiss the parish clerk and sexton or any persons performing or assisting to perform the duties of parish clerk or sexton and to determine their salaries and the conditions of the tenure of their offices or of their employment but subject to the rights of any persons holding the said offices at the appointed day;

(iv) power jointly with the minister to determine the objects to which all moneys to be given or collected in church shall be allocated;

(v) power to make representations to the bishop with regard to any matter affecting the welfare of the church in the parish.

5   **Financial statements of the council**

(1) Every council shall furnish to the annual parochial church meeting for discussion the financial statements of the council for the financial year immediately preceding the meeting.

(2) The financial year referred to in subsection (1) above shall be such period as may be prescribed and the financial statements referred to in that subsection shall be prepared in the prescribed form, audited or independently examined as prescribed and published and displayed in the prescribed manner.

(3) In subsection (2) above 'prescribed' means prescribed by the Church Representation Rules or by regulations made under those Rules.

The Charities Act 2011: Part 8 – Charity Accounts, reports and returns

CHAPTER 1: INDIVIDUAL ACCOUNTS

130   Accounting records

(1)   The charity trustees of a charity must ensure that accounting records are kept in respect of the charity which are sufficient to show and explain all the charity's transactions, and which are such as to

(a) disclose at any time, with reasonable accuracy, the financial position of the charity at that time, and

(b) enable the trustees to ensure that, where any statements of accounts are prepared by them under section 132(1), those statements of accounts comply with the requirements of regulations under section 132(1).

Origin: 1993 s.41(1)

(2)   The accounting records must in particular contain –

(a) entries showing from day to day all sums of money received and expended by the charity, and the matters in respect of which the receipt and expenditure takes place, and

(b) a record of the assets and liabilities of the charity.

Origin: 1993 s.41(2)

131   Preservation of accounting records

(1)   The charity trustees of a charity must preserve any accounting records made for the purposes of section 130 in respect of the charity for at least 6 years from the end of the financial year of the charity in which they are made.

Origin: 1993 s.41(3)

(2)   Subsection (3) applies where a charity ceases to exist within the period of 6 years mentioned in subsection (1) as it applies to any accounting records.

Origin: 1993 s.41(4) (part)

(3)   The obligation to preserve the accounting records in accordance with subsection (1) must continue to be discharged by the last charity trustees of the charity, unless the Commission consents in writing to the records being destroyed or otherwise disposed of.

Origin: 1993 s.41(4)(pt); 2006 Sch.8 para.132(pt)

132   Preparation of statement of accounts

(1)   The charity trustees of a charity must (subject to section 133) prepare in respect of each financial year of the charity a statement of accounts complying with such requirements as to its form and contents as may be prescribed by regulations made by the Minister.

Origin: 1993 s.42(1); SI 2006/2951 Sch.0 para.4(q)

(2)   Regulations under subsection (1) may in particular make provision –

(a)   for any such statement to be prepared in accordance with such methods and principles as are specified or referred to in the regulations;

(b)   as to any information to be provided by way of notes to the accounts.

Origin: 1993 s.42(2) (part)

(3)   Regulations under subsection (1) may also make provision for determining the financial years of a charity for the purposes of this Act and any regulations made under it.

Origin: 1993 s.42(2) (part)

(4)   But regulations under subsection (1) may not impose on the charity trustees of a charity that is a charitable trust created by any person ('the settlor') any requirement to disclose, in any statement of accounts prepared by them under subsection (1) –

(a)   the identities of recipients of grants made out of the funds of the charity, or

(b)   the amounts of any individual grants so made,

if the disclosure would fall to be made at a time when the settlor or any spouse or civil partner of the settlor was still alive.

Origin: 1993 s.42(2A); 2006 Sch.8 para.133(2)

133   Account and statement an option for lower-income charities

If a charity's gross income in any financial year does not exceed £250,000, the charity trustees may, in respect of that year, elect to prepare –

(a)   a receipts and payments account, and

(b)   a statement of assets and liabilities, instead of a statement of accounts under section 132(1).

Origin: 1993 s.42(3); SI 2009/508 art.9

134   Preservation of statement of accounts or account and statement

(1)   The charity trustees of a charity must preserve –

(a)   any statement of accounts prepared by them under section 132(1), or

(b)   any account and statement prepared by them under section 133,

for at least 6 years from the end of the financial year to which any such statement relates or (as the case may be) to which any such account and statement relate.

Origin: 1993 s.42(4)

(2)   Subsection (3) applies if a charity ceases to exist within the period of 6 years 5 mentioned in subsection (1) as it applies to any statement of accounts or account and statement.

Origin: 1993 s.41(4) (part), s.42(5) (part)

(3)   The obligation to preserve the statement or account and statement in accordance with subsection (1) must continue to be discharged by the last 10 charity trustees of the charity, unless the Commission consents in writing to the statement or account and statement being destroyed or otherwise disposed of.

Origin: 1993 s.41(4) (part), s.42(5) (part)

CHAPTER 2: GROUP ACCOUNTS

137   Accounting records

(1)   The charity trustees of a parent charity or of any charity which is a subsidiary undertaking must ensure that the accounting records kept in respect of the charity under –

(a)   s.130(1) (individual accounts: accounting records), or (as the case may be)

(b)   s.386, Companies Act 2006 (c. 46) (duty to keep accounting records),

are such as to enable the charity trustees of the parent charity to ensure that, where any group accounts are prepared by them under s.138(2), those accounts comply with the requirements of regulations under s.142.

Origin: 1993 Sch.5A para.2(1) (part); 2006 Sch.6 (part); SI 2008/527 art.8(3) (part); SI 2008/948 Sch.1 para.192(10) (c) (part)

(2)   The duty in s.137(1) is in addition to the duty to ensure that the accounting records comply with the requirements of (a) s.130(1), or (b) s.386, Companies Act 2006.

Origin: 1993 Sch.5A para.2(1) (part); 2006 Sch.6 (part); SI 2008/527 art.8(3) (part); SI 2008/948 Sch.1 para.192(10) (c) (part)

(3)   S.137(4) applies if a parent charity has a subsidiary undertaking in relation to which the requirements of (a) s.130(1), or (b) s.386, Companies Act 2006, do not apply.

Origin: 1993 Sch.5A para.2(2) (pt), (3) (pt); 2006 Sch.6 (pt); SI 2008/527 art.8(3); SI 2008/948 Sch.1 para.192(10)(c) (pt)

(4)   The charity trustees of the parent charity must take reasonable steps to secure that the undertaking keeps such accounting records as to enable the trustees to ensure that, where any group accounts are prepared by them under s.138(2), those accounts comply with the requirements of regulations under s.142.

Origin: 1993 Sch.5A para.2(2) (pt), (3) (pt); 2006 Sch.6 (pt)

138   Preparation of group accounts

(1)   This section applies in relation to a financial year of a charity if –

(a)   the charity is a parent charity at the end of that year, and

(b)   (where it is a company) it is not required to prepare consolidated accounts for that year under s.399, Companies Act 2006 (duty to prepare group accounts), whether or not such accounts are in fact prepared.

Origin: 1993 Sch.5A para.3(1); SI 2008/527 art.8(4); SI 2008/948 Sch.1 para.192(10)(d)

(2)   The charity trustees of the parent charity must prepare group accounts in respect of that year.

Origin: 1993 Sch.5A para.3(2); 2006 Sch.6 (part)

(3)   If the requirement in s.138(2) applies to the charity trustees of a parent charity (other than a parent charity which is a company) in relation to a financial year –

(a)   that requirement so applies in addition to the requirement in s.132(1) (statement of accounts), and

(b)   the option of preparing the documents mentioned in s.133 (account and statement) is not available in relation to that year (whatever the amount of the charity.s gross income for that year).

Origin: 1993 Sch.5A para.3(6); 2006 Sch.6 (part); SI 2008/527 art.8(5)

(4)   If (a) the requirement in s.138(2) applies to the charity trustees of a parent charity in relation to a financial year and (b) the charity is a company, that requirement so applies in addition to the requirement in s.394, Companies Act 2006 (c. 46) (duty to prepare individual accounts).

Origin: 1993 Sch.5A para.3(6A); SI 2008/527 art.8(6); SI 2008/948 Sch.1 para.192(10)(d)

(5)   S.138(2) is subject to s.139. Origin: 1993 Sch.5A para.3(7); 2006 Sch.6 (part)

139   Exceptions to requirement to prepare group accounts

(1)   The requirement in s.138(2) does not apply to the charity trustees of a parent charity in relation to a financial year if at the end of that year it is itself a subsidiary undertaking in relation to another charity.

Origin: 1993 Sch.5A para.4(1); 2006 Sch.6 (part)

(2)   The requirement in s.138(2) does not apply to the charity trustees of a parent charity in relation to a financial year if the aggregate gross income of the group for that year does not exceed such sum as is specified in regulations made by the Minister.

Origin: 1993 Sch.5A para.4(2); 2006 Sch.6 (part)

(3)   Regulations made by the Minister may prescribe circumstances in which a subsidiary undertaking may or (as the case may be) must be excluded from group accounts required to be prepared under s.138(2) for a financial year.

Origin: 1993 Sch.5A para.4(3); 2006 Sch.6 (part)

(4)   Where, by virtue of such regulations, each of the subsidiary undertakings which are members of a group is (a) permitted to be excluded from any such group accounts for a financial year or (b) required to be so excluded, the requirement in s.138(2) does not apply to the charity trustees of the parent charity in relation to that year. *Origin: 1993 Sch.5A para.4(4); 2006 Sch.6 (part)*

140   Preservation of group accounts

(1)   The charity trustees of a charity must preserve any group accounts prepared by them under s.138(2) for at least 6 years from the end of the financial year to which the accounts relate.

Origin: 1993 Sch.5A para.5(1); 2006 Sch.6 (part)

(2)   S.140(3) applies if a charity ceases to exist within the period of 6 years mentioned in s.140(1) as it applies to any group accounts.

Origin: 1993 s.41(4) (part), Sch.5A para.5(2) (part); 2006 Sch.6 (part)

(3)   The obligation to preserve the accounts in accordance with s.140(1) must continue to be discharged by the last charity trustees of the charity, unless the Commission consents in writing to the accounts being destroyed, or otherwise disposed of.

Origin: 1993 s.41(4) (part), Sch.5A para.5(2) (part); 2006 Sch.6 (part)

141   'Parent charity', 'subsidiary undertaking' and 'group'

(1)   This section applies for the purposes of this Part. *Origin: 1993 Sch.5A para.1(1); 2006 Sch.6 (part)*

(2)   A charity is a 'parent charity' if it is (or is to be treated as) a parent undertaking in relation to one or more other undertakings in accordance with the provisions of s.1162 of, and Sch. 7 to, the Companies Act 2006 (c. 46).

Origin: 1993 Sch.5A para.1(2); SI 2008/527 art.8(2); SI 2008/948 Sch.1 para.192(10)(a)

(3)   Each undertaking in relation to which a parent charity is (or is to be treated as) a parent undertaking in accordance with those provisions is a 'subsidiary undertaking' in relation to the parent charity.

Origin: 1993 Sch.5A para.1(3); 2006 Sch.6 (part)

(4)   But subsection (3) does not have the result that any of the following is a 'subsidiary undertaking' –

    (a)   any special trusts of a charity,

    (b)   any institution which, by virtue of a direction under s.12(1), is to be treated as forming part of a charity for the purposes of this Part, or

    (c)   any charity to which a direction under s.12(2) applies for the purposes of this Part.

Origin: 1993 Sch.5A para.1(4); 2006 Sch.6 (part)

(5)   'The group', in relation to a parent charity, means that charity and its subsidiary undertaking or undertakings, and any reference to the members of the group is to be read accordingly.

Origin: 1993 Sch.5A para.1(5); 2006 Sch.6 (part)

(6)   For the purposes of this section and the operation for those purposes of s.1162 of, and Sch. 7 to, the Companies Act 2006 (c. 46) 'undertaking' means (a) an undertaking as defined by s.1161(1) of the 2006 Act or (b) a charity which is not an undertaking as so defined.

Origin: 1993 Sch.5A para.1(6), (7); 2006 Sch.6 (part); SI 2008/948 Sch.1 para.192(10)(b)

142 **'Group accounts'**

(1)   For the purposes of this Part, 'group accounts' means consolidated accounts –

    (a)   relating to the group, and

    (b)   complying with such requirements as to their form and contents as may be prescribed by regulations made by the Minister.

Origin: 1993 Sch.5A para.3(3); 2006 Sch.6 (part)

(2)   Regulations under s.142(1) may in particular make provision –

    (a)   for any such accounts to be prepared in accordance with such methods and principles as are specified or referred to in the regulations;

    (b)   for dealing with cases where the financial years of the members of the group do not all coincide;

    (c)   as to any information to be provided by way of notes to the accounts.

Origin: 1993 Sch.5A para.3(4); 2006 Sch.6 (part)

(3)   Regulations under subsection (1) may also make provision –

    (a)   for determining the financial years of subsidiary undertakings for the purposes of this Chapter;

    (b)   for imposing on the charity trustees of a parent charity requirements with respect to securing that such financial years coincide with that of the charity.

Origin: 1993 Sch.5A para.3(5); 2006 Sch.6 (part)

CHAPTER 3: AUDIT OR EXAMINATION OF ACCOUNTS

Audit or examination of individual accounts

144 **Audit of accounts of larger charities**

(1)   S.144(2) applies to a financial year of a charity if –

    (a) the charity's gross income in that year exceeds £500,000, or

    (b) the charity's gross income in that year exceeds the accounts threshold and at the end of the year the aggregate value of its assets (before deduction of liabilities) exceeds £3.26 million. 'The accounts threshold' means the sum for the time being specified in s.133 (account and statement an option for lower-income charities).

Origin: 1993 s.43(1); 2006 s.28(2); SI 2009/508 art.10 (part); Pre-consolidation Order Sch.0 para.16

(2)   If this subsection applies to a financial year of a charity, the accounts of the charity for that year must be audited by a person who –

    (a) is eligible for appointment as a statutory auditor under Part 42 of the Companies Act 2006 (c. 46), or

    (b) is a member of a body for the time being specified in regulations under s.154 and is under the rules of that body eligible for appointment as auditor of the charity.

Origin: 1993 s.43(2); SI 2008/948 Sch.1 para.17

145 **Examination of accounts an option for lower-income charities**

(1)   If s.144(2) does not apply to a financial year of a charity but its gross income in that year exceeds £25,000, the accounts of the charity for that year must, at the election of the charity trustees –

    (a) be examined by an independent examiner, that is, an independent person who is reasonably believed by the trustees to have the requisite ability and practical experience to carry out a competent examination of the accounts, or

(b) be audited by a person within s.144(2)(a) or (b).

Origin: 1993 s.43(3) (part); 2006 s.28(4) (part); SI 2009/508 art.10 (part)

(2)   S.145(1) is subject to (a) s.145(3, and (b) any order under s.146(1).

Origin: 1993 s.43(3) (part); 2006 s.28(4) (part)

(3)   If s.145(1) applies to the accounts of a charity for a year and the charity's gross income in that year exceeds £250,000, a person qualifies as an independent examiner for the purposes of s.145(1)(a) if (and only if) the person is independent and (a) a member of one of the bodies listed in s.145(4) or (b) a Fellow of the Association of Charity Independent Examiners.

Origin: 1993 s.43(3A); 2006 s.28(5); SI 2008/527 art.2(3)

(4)   The bodies referred to in subsection (3)(a) are –

(a)   the Institute of Chartered Accountants in England and Wales;

(b)   the Institute of Chartered Accountants of Scotland;

(c)   the Institute of Chartered Accountants in Ireland;

(d)   the Association of Chartered Certified Accountants;

(e)   the Association of Authorised Public Accountants;

(f)   the Association of Accounting Technicians;

(g)   the Association of International Accountants;

(h)   the Chartered Institute of Management Accountants;

(i)   the Institute of Chartered Secretaries and Administrators;

(j)   the Chartered Institute of Public Finance and Accountancy.

Origin: 1993 s.43(3B); SI 2008/527 art.2(4)

(5)   The Commission may –

(a)   give guidance to charity trustees in connection with the selection of a person for appointment as an independent examiner;

(b)   give such directions as it thinks appropriate with respect to the carrying out of an examination in pursuance of s.145(1)(a);

and any such guidance or directions may either be of general application or apply to a particular charity only.

Origin: 1993 s.43(7) (part); 2006 Sch.8 para.134(5) (part)

(6)   The Minister may by order –

(a)   amend s.145(3) by adding or removing a description of person to or from the list in that subsection or by varying any entry for the time being included in that list;

(b)   amend s.145(4) by adding or removing a body to or from the list in that subsection or by varying any entry for the time being included in that list.

Origin: 1993 s.43(8) (part); 2006 s.28(6) (part); SI 2008/527 art.2(5)

146   Commission's powers to order audit

(1)   The Commission may by order require the accounts of a charity for a financial year to be audited by a person within s.144(2)(a) or (b) if it appears to the Commission that –

(a) 144(2), or (as the case may be) s.145(1), has not been complied with in relation to that year within 10 months from the end of that year, or

(b) although s.144(2) does not apply to that year, it would nevertheless be desirable for the accounts of the charity for that year to be audited by a person within s.144(2)(a) or (b).

Origin: 1993 s.43(4) (part); 2006 Sch.8 para.134(2) (part)

(2) If the Commission makes an order under s.146(1) with respect to a charity, the auditor must be a person appointed by the Commission unless –

(a) the order is made by virtue of s.146(1)(b), and

(b) the charity trustees themselves appoint an auditor in accordance with the order.

Origin: 1993 s.43(5) (part); 2006 Sch.8 para.134(3) (part)

(3) The expenses of any audit carried out by an auditor appointed by the Commission under s.146(2), including the auditor's remuneration, are recoverable by the Commission:

(a) from the charity trustees of the charity concerned, who are personally liable, jointly and severally, for those expenses, or

(b) to the extent that it appears to the Commission not to be practical to seek recovery of those expenses in accordance with paragraph (a), from the funds of the charity.

Origin: 1993 s.43(6) (part); 2006 Sch.8 para.134(4) (part)

Audit or examination of group accounts

151 Audit of accounts of larger groups

(1) This section applies where group accounts are prepared for a financial year of a parent charity under s.138(2) and –

(a) the aggregate gross income of the group in that year exceeds the relevant income threshold, or

(b) the aggregate gross income of the group in that year exceeds the relevant income threshold and at the end of the year the aggregate value of the assets of the group (before deduction of liabilities) exceeds the relevant assets threshold.

Origin: 1993 Sch.5A para.6(1); 2006 Sch.6 (part)

(2) This section also applies where –

(a) group accounts are prepared for a financial year of a parent charity under s.138(2), and

(b) the appropriate audit provision applies in relation to the parent charity's own accounts for that year.

Origin: 1993 Sch.5A para.6(3); 2006 Sch.6 (part)

(3) In this section 'the appropriate audit provision', in relation to a financial year of a parent charity, means –

(a) (subject to para.(b), (c) or (d)) s.144(2) (audit of accounts of larger charities); ...

Origin: 1993 Sch.5A para.6(9); 2006 Sch.6 (part)

(4) If this section applies in relation to a financial year of a parent charity by virtue of s.151(1) or (2), the group accounts for that year must be audited –

(a) ... by a person within s.144(2)(a) or (b);

Origin: 1993 Sch.5A para.6(4); 2006 Sch.6 (part)

(5)   If this section applies in relation to a financial year of a parent charity by virtue of s.151(1) –

(a)   (subject to para.(b)) the appropriate audit provision applies in relation to the parent charity's own accounts for that year (whether or not it would otherwise so apply); ...

Origin: 1993 Sch.5A para.6(8)

(6)   S.149(4) & (6) apply in relation to any appointment under s.151(4)(b) as they apply in relation to an appointment under s.149(2).

Origin: 1993 Sch.5A para.6(7); 2006 Sch.6 (pt)

152   Examination of accounts an option for smaller groups

(1)   This section applies if –

(a)   group accounts are prepared for a financial year of a parent charity under s.138(2), and

(b)   s.151 (audit of accounts of larger groups) does not apply in relation to that year.

Origin: 1993 Sch.5A para.7(1); 2006 Sch.6 (part)

(2)   If (a) this section applies in relation to a financial year of a parent charity, (b) the aggregate gross income of the group in that year exceeds the sum specified in s.145(1), and (c) s.152(6) or (7) (audit of NHS charity accounts) does not apply in relation to it, the group accounts for that year must, at the election of the charity trustees of the parent charity, be examined by an independent examiner (as defined in s.145(1)) or audited by a person within s.144(2)(a) or (b).

Origin: 1993 s.43(3) (part), Sch.5A para.7(2) (part), (3) (part); 2006 Sch.6 (part)

(3)   S.152(2) is subject to (a) s.152(4) and (b) any order under s.153(1).

Origin: 1993 s.43(3) (part), Sch.5A para.7(2) (part), (3) (part); 2006 Sch.6 (part)

(4)   If s.152(2) applies to the group accounts for a year and the aggregate gross income of the group in that year exceeds the sum specified in s.145(3), a person qualifies as an independent examiner for the purposes of s.152(2)(a) if (and only if) the person is independent and meets the requirements of s.145(3)(a) or (b).

Origin: 1993 s.43(3A) (part), Sch.5A para.7(2) (part), (3) (part); 2006 Sch.6 (part)

(5)   The Commission may (a) give guidance to charity trustees of the parent charity in connection with the selection of a person for appointment as an independent examiner; (b) give such directions as it thinks appropriate with respect to the carrying out of an examination in pursuance of s.152(2); and any such guidance or directions may either be of general application or apply to a particular charity only.

Origin: 1993 s.43(7) (part), Sch.5A para.7(2) (part), (3) (part); 2006 Sch.6 (part), Sch.8 para.134(5) (part)

(8)   If the group accounts for a financial year of a parent charity are to be examined or audited in accordance with s.152(2), s.145(1) applies in relation to the parent charity's own accounts for that year (whether or not it would otherwise so apply).

Origin: 1993 Sch.5A para.7(6); 2006 Sch.6 (part)

(9)   Nothing in s.152(6) or (7) affects the operation of s.149(3)-(6) or (as the case may be) s.150(3) in relation to the parent charity's own accounts for the financial year in question.

Origin: 1993 Sch.5A para.7(7); 2006 Sch.6 (part)

153   Commission's powers to order audit of group accounts

(1)   The Commission may by order require the group accounts for a year to be audited by a person within s.144(2)(a) or (b) if it appears to the Commission that –

(a)   s.151(4)(a), or (as the case may be) s.152(2), has not been complied with in relation to that year within 10 months from the end of that year, or

    (b)   although s.151 does not apply to a financial year of a parent charity, it would nevertheless be desirable for the group accounts for that year to be audited by a person within s.144(2)(a) or (b).

Origin: 1993 s.43(4) (part), Sch.5A paras.6(5) (part), 7(2) (part), (3) (part); 2006 Sch.6 (part), Sch.8 para.134(2) (part)

(2)   If the Commission makes an order under s.153(1) with respect to group accounts, the auditor must be a person appointed by the Commission unless (a) the order is made by virtue of s.153(1)(b), and (b) the charity trustees of the parent charity themselves appoint an auditor in accordance with the order.

Origin: 1993 s.43(5) (part), Sch.5A paras.6(5) (part), 7(2) (part), (3) (part); 2006 Sch.6 (part), Sch.8 para.134(3) (part)

(3)   The expenses of any audit carried out by an auditor appointed by the Commission under s.153(2), including the auditor's remuneration, are recoverable by the Commission –

    (a)   from the charity trustees of the parent charity, who are personally liable, jointly and severally, for those expenses, or

    (b)   to the extent that it appears to the Commission not to be practical to seek recovery of those expenses in accordance with paragraph (a), from the funds of the parent charity.

Origin: 1993 s.43(6) (part), Sch.5A paras.6(6), 7(2) (part), (3) (part); 2006 Sch.6 (part), Sch.8 para.134(4) (part)

Regulations relating to audits and examinations

154   Regulations relating to audits and examinations

(1)   The Minister may by regulations make provision –

    (a)   specifying one or more bodies for the purposes of s.144(2)(b);

    (b)   with respect to the duties of an auditor carrying out an audit of individual or group accounts, including provision with respect to the making by the auditor of a report on –

        (i)   the statement of accounts prepared for the financial year in question under s.132(1),

        (ii)   the account and statement so prepared under s.133,

        (iii)   the accounts so prepared under s.394 of the Companies Act 2006 (c. 46) (duty to prepare individual accounts), or

        (iv)   group accounts so prepared under section 138(2), as the case may be;

    (c)   with respect to the making of a report in respect of an examination of individual or group accounts by the independent examiner or examiner who has carried out the examination;

    (d)   conferring on such an auditor or on an independent examiner or examiner a right of access with respect to books, documents and other records (however kept) which relate (i) to the charity concerned or (ii) in the case of an audit or examination of group accounts, to any member of the group;

    (e)   entitling such an auditor or an independent examiner or examiner to require, in the case of a charity, information and explanations from –

        (i)   past or present charity trustees or trustees for the charity or, in the case of an audit or examination of group accounts, for any member of the group, or

        (ii)   past or present officers or employees of the charity or, in the case of an audit or examination of group accounts, of any member of the group;

    (f)   enabling the Commission, in circumstances specified in the regulations, to dispense with the requirements of s.144(2), s.145(1), s.151(4)(a) or s.152(2) –

        (i)   in the case of a particular charity, or

(ii) in the case of any particular financial year of a charity.

Origin 1993 s.44(1)(pt), Sch.5A para.8(1)(pt), (2) (pt); 2006 Sch.8 para.137(2) (pt); SI 2006/2951 Sch.0 para.4(s); SI 2008/527 art.3; SI 2008/948 Sch.1 para.192(5); Pre-consolidation Order Sch.0 para.29(1)

(2) Regulations under s.154(1)(e) may in particular make, in relation to audits or examinations of group accounts, provision corresponding or similar to any provision made by s.499 or s.500 of the Companies Act 2006 (c. 46) in connection with the rights exercisable by an auditor of a company in relation to a subsidiary undertaking of the company.

Origin: 1993 Sch.5A para.8(3); 2006 Sch.6(pt); SI 2008/948 Sch.1 para.192(10)(f)

(3) In this section –

'audit of individual or group accounts' means an audit under –

(a) s.144, 145, 146, 149 or 150 (individual accounts), or

(b) s.151, 152 or 153 (group accounts);

'examination of individual or group accounts' means an examination under –

(a) s.145, 149 or 150 (individual accounts), or

(b) s.152(2) or 152(6) or (7) (group accounts);

'audit or examination of group accounts' means an audit or examination under s.151, 152 or 153.

Origin: 1993 s.44(1) (part), Sch.5A para.8(1) (part), (2) (part); 2006 Sch.8 para.137(2) (part); drafting

155   Power of Commission to direct compliance with certain regulations

If any person fails to afford an auditor or an independent examiner or examiner any facility to which the auditor, independent examiner or examiner is entitled by virtue of s.154(1)(d) or (e), the Commission may by order give (a) to that person or (b) to the charity trustees for the time being of the charity concerned, such directions as the Commission thinks appropriate for securing that the default is made good.

Origin: 1993 s.44(2), Sch.5A para.8(4); 2006 Sch.8 para.137(3)

Duty of auditors etc. to report matters to Commission

156   Duty of auditors etc. to report matters to Commission

(1) This section applies to a person ('P') who –

(a) is acting as an auditor or independent examiner appointed by or in relation to a charity under s.144 to 146 (audit or examination of individual accounts), ...

(2) If, in the course of acting in the capacity mentioned in s.156(1), P becomes aware of a matter –

(a) which relates to the activities or affairs of the charity or of any connected institution or body, and

(b) which P has reasonable cause to believe is likely to be of material significance for the purposes of the exercise by the Commission of its functions under the provisions mentioned in s.156(3),

P must immediately make a written report on the matter to the Commission.

Origin: 1993 s.44A(2) (part); 2006 s.29(1) (part)

(3) The provisions are –

(a) s.46, 47 and 50 (inquiries by Commission);

(b) s.76, 79, 80, 81 and 82 (Commission's powers to act for protection of charities).

Origin: 1993 s.44A(2) (part); 2006 s.29(1) (part)

(4)   If, in the course of acting in the capacity mentioned in s.156(1), P becomes aware of any matter –

(a)   which does not appear to P to be one that P is required to report under s.156(2), but

(b)   which P has reasonable cause to believe is likely to be relevant for the purposes of the exercise by the Commission of any of its functions,

P may make a report on the matter to the Commission.

Origin: 1993 s.44A(3); 2006 s.29(1) (part)

(5)   Where the duty or power under s.156(2) or (4) has arisen in relation to P when acting in the capacity mentioned in s.156(1), the duty or power is not affected by P's subsequently ceasing to act in that capacity. *Origin: 1993 s.44A(4); 2006 s.29(1) (part)*

(6)   Where P makes a report as required or authorised by s.156(2) or (4), no duty to which P is subject is to be regarded as contravened merely because of any information or opinion contained in the report.

Origin: 1993 s.44A(5); 2006 s.29(1) (part)

157   Meaning of 'connected institution or body' in s.156(2)

(1)   In s.156(2) 'connected institution or body', in relation to a charity, means –

(a)   an institution which is controlled by, or

(b)   a body corporate in which a substantial interest is held by, the charity or any one or more of the charity trustees acting as such.

Origin: 1993 s.44A(6); 2006 s.29(1) (part)

(2)   S.351 and s.352 (meaning of controlled institution and substantial interest) apply for the purposes of s.157(1).

Origin: 1993 s.44A(7); 2006 s.29(1) (part)

158   Application of duty in relation to group accounts

(1)   S.156(2)-(6) apply in relation to a person appointed to audit, or report on, any group accounts under or by virtue of s.151 to 153 as they apply in relation to a person such as is mentioned in s.156(1). Origin: 1993 Sch.5A para.9(1); 2006 Sch.6 (part) (2) In s.156(2)(a), as it applies in accordance with s.158(1), the reference to the charity or any connected institution or body is to be read as a reference to the parent charity or any of its subsidiary undertakings.

Origin: 1993 Sch.5A para.9(2); 2006 Sch.6 (part)

Exempt and excepted charities

161   Excepted charities [93s046_3]   ?

(1)   Nothing in s.144 to s.146 (audit or examination of individual accounts) applies to any charity which (a) falls within s.30(2)(d) (whether or not it also falls within s.30(2)(b) or (c)) and (b) is not registered.

Origin: 1993 s.46(3) (part); 2006 Sch.8 para.139(3) (part)

(2)   Except in accordance with s.161(3) and (4), nothing in –

(a)   s.154 or s.155 (regulations relating to audits and examinations), or

(b)   s.156 or s.157 (duty of auditors etc. to report matters to Commission),

applies to a charity mentioned in s.161(1).

Origin: 1993 s.46(3) (part); 2006 Sch.8 para.139(3) (part)

CHAPTER 4: ANNUAL REPORTS AND RETURNS AND PUBLIC ACCESS TO ACCOUNTS ETC.

Annual reports etc.

162   Charity trustees to prepare annual reports

(1)   The charity trustees of a charity must prepare in respect of each financial year of the charity an annual report containing –

    (a)   such a report by the trustees on the activities of the charity during that year, and

    (b)   such other information relating to the charity or to its trustees or officers,

as may be prescribed by regulations made by the Minister.

Origin: 1993 s.45(1); SI 2006/2951 Sch.0 para.4(t)

(2)   Regulations under s.162(1) may in particular make provision –

    (a)   for any such report as is mentioned in s.162(1)(a) to be prepared in accordance with such principles as are specified or referred to in the regulations;

    (b)   enabling the Commission to dispense with any requirement prescribed by virtue of s.162(1)(b) (i) in the case of a particular charity or a particular class of charities, or (ii) in the case of a particular financial year of a charity or of any class of charities.

Origin: 1993 s.45(2); 2006 Sch.8 para.138(2)

163   Transmission of annual reports to Commission in certain cases

(1)   Where a charity's gross income in any financial year exceeds £25,000, a copy of the annual report required to be prepared under s.162 in respect of that year must be transmitted to the Commission by the charity trustees within (a) 10 months from the end of that year or (b) such longer period as the Commission may for any special reason allow in the case of that report.

Origin: 1993 s.45(3); DCOA 1994 s.29(1); 2006 Sch.8 para.138(3); SI 2009/508 art.11 (part)

(2)   Where a charity's gross income in any financial year does not exceed £25,000, the annual report required to be prepared under s.162 in respect of that year must, if the Commission so requests, be transmitted to it by the charity trustees –

    (a)   in the case of a request made before the end of 7 months from the end of the financial year to which the report relates, within 10 months from the end of that year, and

    (b)   in the case of a request not so made, within 3 months from the date of the request,

or, in either case, within such longer period as the Commission may for any special reason allow in the case of that report.

Origin: 1993 s.45(3A); DCOA 1994 s.29(2); 2006 Sch.8 para.138(4); SI 2009/508 art.11 (part)

(3)   In the case of a charity which is constituted as a CIO (a) the requirement imposed by s.163(1) applies whatever the charity's gross income is and (b) s.163 (2) does not apply.

Origin: 1993 s.45(3B); 2006 Sch.7 para.4

164   Documents to be transmitted with annual report

(1)   Subject to s.164(3), any copy of an annual report transmitted to the Commission under s.163 must have attached to it –

    (a)   a copy of the statement of accounts prepared for the financial year in question under s.132(1), or

    (b)   (as the case may be) a copy of the account and statement so prepared under s.133, and a copy of the relevant auditor's or examiner's report.

Origin: 1993 s.45(4) (part); DCOA 1994 s.29(3); 2006 Sch.8 para.138(5); drafting

(2)   In s.164(1), 'the relevant auditor's or examiner's report' means –

(a) if the accounts of the charity for that year have been audited under s.144, 145, 146, 149 or 150, the report made by the auditor on that statement of accounts or (as the case may be) on that account and statement;

(b) if the accounts of the charity for that year have been examined under s.145, 149 or 150, the report made by the person carrying out the examination.

Origin: 1993 s.45(4) (part); SI 2005/1074 art.3(4) (part)

165   Preservation of annual reports etc.

(1)   Any copy of an annual report transmitted to the Commission under s.163, together with the documents attached to it, is to be kept by the Commission for such period as it thinks fit.

Origin: 1993 s.45(6); DCOA 1994 s.29(5); 2006 Sch.8 para.138(7)

(2)   The charity trustees of a charity must preserve for at least 6 years from the end of the financial year to which it relates an annual report prepared by them under s.162(1) if they have not been required to transmit a copy of it to the Commission.

Origin: 1993 s.45(7); DCOA 1994 s.29(6) (part); 2006 Sch.8 para.138(8)

(3)   S.165(4) applies if a charity ceases to exist within the period of 6 years mentioned in s.165(2) as it applies to any annual report.

Origin: 1993 s.41(4) (part), s.45(8) (part); DCOA 1994 s.29(6) (part); 2006 Sch.8 para.138(9) (part)

(4)   The obligation to preserve the annual report in accordance with s.165(2) must continue to be discharged by the last charity trustees of the charity, unless the Commission consents in writing to the annual report being destroyed or otherwise disposed of.

Origin: 1993 s.41(4) (part), s.45(8) (part); DCOA 1994 s.29(6) (part); 2006 Sch.8 para.138(9) (part)

166   Annual reports and group accounts

(1)   This section applies where group accounts are prepared for a financial year of a parent charity under s.138(2). *Origin: 1993 Sch.5A para.10(1); 2006 Sch.6 (part)*

(2)   The annual report prepared by the charity trustees of the parent charity in respect of that year under s.162 must include –

(a) such a report by the trustees on the activities of the charity's subsidiary undertakings during that year, and

(b) such other information relating to any of those undertakings,

as may be prescribed by regulations made by the Minister.

Origin: 1993 Sch.5A para.10(2); 2006 Sch.6 (part)

(3)   Regulations under s.166(2) may in particular make provision –

(a) for any such report as is mentioned in s.166(2)(a) to be prepared in accordance with such principles as are specified or referred to in the regulations;

(b) enabling the Commission to dispense with any requirement prescribed by virtue of s.166(2)(b) in the case of (i) a particular subsidiary undertaking or (ii) a particular class of subsidiary undertaking.

Origin: 1993 Sch.5A para.10(3); 2006 Sch.6 (part) (4) S.163

(transmission of annual report to Commission in certain cases) applies in relation to the annual report referred to in s.166(2) as if any reference to the charity's gross income in the financial year in question were a reference to the aggregate gross income of the group in that year.

Origin: 1993 Sch.5A para.10(4); 2006 Sch.6 (part)

(5)   When transmitted to the Commission in accordance with s.166(4), the copy of the annual report must have attached to it both a copy of the group accounts prepared for that year under s.138(2), and

(a) a copy of the report made by the auditor on those accounts, or

(b) if those accounts have been examined under s.152, a copy of the report made by the person carrying out the examination.

Origin: 1993 Sch.5A para.10(5); 2006 Sch.6 (part)

(6)   The requirements in this section are in addition to those in s.162 to s.165.

Origin: 1993 Sch.5A para.10(6); 2006 Sch.6 (part)

168   Excepted charities

(1)   Nothing in s.162 to s.165 (annual reports etc.) applies to any charity which (a) falls within s.30(2)(d) (whether or not it also falls within s.30(2)(b) or (c)) and (b) is not registered.

Origin: 1993 s.46(3) (part); 2006 Sch.8 para.139(3) (part)

(2)   Except in accordance with s.168(5), nothing in s.162 to s.165 applies to any charity which (a) falls within s.30(2)(b) or (c) but does not fall within s.30(2)(d) and (b) is not registered.

Origin: 1993 s.46(4); 2006 Sch.8 para.139(4)

(3)   If requested to do so by the Commission, the charity trustees of any such charity as is mentioned in s.168(2) must prepare an annual report in respect of such financial year of the charity as is specified in the Commission's request. *Origin: 1993 s.46(5); 2006 Sch.8 para.139(5)*

(4)   Any report prepared under s.168(3) must contain –

(a) such a report by the charity trustees on the activities of the charity during the year in question, and

(b) such other information relating to the charity or to its trustees or officers, as may be prescribed by regulations made under s.162(1) in relation to annual reports prepared under that provision.

Origin: 1993 s.46(6)

(5)   The following provisions apply in relation to any report required to be prepared under s.168(3) as if it were an annual report required to be prepared under s.162(1) –

(a) s.163(1) (transmission of annual report in certain cases), with the omission of the words preceding 'a copy of the annual report', and

(b) s.164 (documents to be transmitted with annual report) and s.165(1) (preservation of annual report).

Origin: 1993 s.46(7); 2006 Sch.8 para.139(6) 35

(6)   S.168(7) & (8) apply where –

(a) a charity is required to prepare an annual report in respect of a financial year by virtue of s.168(3),

(b) the charity is a parent charity at the end of the year, and

(c) group accounts are prepared for that year under s.138(2) by the charity trustees of the charity.

Origin: 1993 Sch.5A para.11(1); 2006 Sch.6 (part)

(7)   When transmitted to the Commission in accordance with s.168(5), the copy of the annual report must have attached to it both a copy of the group accounts and –

(a) a copy of the report made by the auditor on those accounts, or

(b) where those accounts have been examined under s.152, a copy of the report made by the person carrying out the examination. *Origin: 1993 Sch.5A para.11(2); 2006 Sch.6 (part)*

(8)   The requirement in s.168(7) is in addition to that in s.168(4).

Origin: 1993 Sch.5A para.11(3); 2006 Sch.6 (part)

Annual returns

169   Annual returns by registered charities

(1)   Subject to s.169(2), every registered charity must prepare in respect of each of its financial years an annual return in such form, and containing such information, as may be prescribed by regulations made by the Commission. *Origin: 1993 s.48(1); DCOA 1994 s.30(2); 2006 Sch.8 para.141(2)*

(2)   S.169(1) does not apply in relation to any financial year of a charity in which the charity's gross income does not exceed £10,000 (but this subsection does not apply if the charity is constituted as a CIO).

Origin: 1993 s.48(1A); DCOA 1994 s.30(3); 2006 Sch.7 para.5, Sch.8 para.141(3)

(3)   Any such return must be transmitted to the Commission by the date by which the charity trustees are, by virtue of s.163(1), required to transmit to the Commission the annual report required to be prepared in respect of the financial year in question. *Origin: 1993 s.48(2); 2006 Sch.8 para.141(4)*

(4)   The Commission may dispense with the requirements of s.169(1) –

(a)   in the case of a particular charity or a particular class of charities, or

(b)   in the case of a particular financial year of a charity or of any class of charities.

Origin: 1993 s.48(3); 2006 Sch.8 para.141(5)

Availability of documents to public

170   Public inspection of annual reports etc. kept by Commission

Any document kept by the Commission in pursuance of s.165(1) (preservation of annual reports and attachments) must be open to public inspection at all reasonable times –

(a)   during the period for which it is so kept, or

(b)   if the Commission so determines, during such lesser period as it may specify.

Origin: 1993 s.47(1); 2006 Sch.8 para.140(2)

171   Supply by charity trustees of copy of most recent annual report

(1)   This section applies if an annual report has been prepared in respect of any financial year of a charity in pursuance of s.162(1) or s.168(3).

Origin: 1993 s.47(2) (part), (4); 2006 Sch.8 para.140(3) (part), (4) (part)

(2)   If the charity trustees of a charity –

(a)   are requested in writing by any person to provide that person with a copy of its most recent annual report, and

(b)   are paid by that person such reasonable fee (if any) as they may require in respect of the costs of complying with the request,

they must comply with the request within the period of 2 months beginning with the date on which it is made. *Origin: 1993 s.47(2) (part); 2006 Sch.8 para.140(3) (part)*

(3)   The reference in s.171(2) to a charity's most recent annual report is a reference to the annual report prepared in pursuance of s.162(1) or s.168(3) in respect of the last financial year of the charity in respect of which an annual report has been so prepared.

Origin: 1993 s.47(5); 2006 Sch.8 para.140(4) (part)

172   Supply by charity trustees of copy of most recent accounts

(1)   If the charity trustees of a charity –

(a)   are requested in writing by any person to provide that person with a copy of the charity's most recent accounts, and

(b)   are paid by that person such reasonable fee (if any) as they may require in respect of the costs of complying with the request,

they must comply with the request within the period of 2 months beginning with the date on which it is made.

Origin: 1993 s.47(2) (part); 2006 Sch.8 para.140(3) (part)

(2)   The reference in s.172(1) to a charity's most recent accounts is –

(a)   in the case of a charity other than one falling within para.(b) or (c), a reference to –

(i) the statement of accounts or account & statement prepared in pursuance of s.132(1), or

(ii) the account & statement prepared in pursuance of s.133,

in respect of the last financial year of the charity in respect of which a statement of accounts or account & statement has or have been so prepared;

(b)   in the case of a charitable company, a reference to the most recent annual accounts of the company prepared under Part 16 of the Companies Act 2006 (c. 46) in relation to which any of the following conditions is satisfied –

(i)   they have been audited,

(ii)   they have been examined by an independent examiner under s.145(1)(a), or

(iii)   they relate to a year in respect of which the company is exempt from audit under Part 16 of the Companies Act 2006 and neither s.144(2) nor s.145(1) applied to them, and

(c)   in the case of an exempt charity, a reference to the accounts of the charity most recently audited in pursuance of any statutory or other requirement or, if its accounts are not required to be audited, the accounts most recently prepared in respect of the charity.

Origin: 1993 s.47(3) (part); DCOA 1994 Sch.11 para.12; SI 1994/1935 Sch.1 para.7 (part); SI 2008/527 art.5; SI 2008/948 Sch.1 para.192(7)

(3)   In s.172(1), the reference to a charity's most recent accounts includes, in relation to a charity whose charity trustees have prepared any group accounts under s.138(2), the group accounts most recently prepared by them. *Origin: 1993 Sch.5A para.13; 2006 Sch.6 (part)*

Offences

173   Offences of failing to supply certain documents

(1)   If any requirement within s.173(2) is not complied with, each person who immediately before the specified date for compliance was a charity trustee of the charity is guilty of an offence.

Origin: 1993 s.49(1) (part), Sch.5A para.14(1) (part); 2006 Sch.8 para.142 (part)

(2)   A requirement is within this subsection if it is imposed –

(a)   by s.163 or by virtue of s.166(4) (requirements to transmit annual report to Commission), taken with s.164, s.166(5) and s.168(7) (documents to be supplied with annual report), as applicable,

(b)   by s.171(2) (supply by charity trustees of copy of most recent annual report),

(c)   by s.172(1) or by virtue of s.172(3) (supply by charity trustees of copy of most recent accounts), or

(d) by s.169(3) (requirement to transmit annual return to Commission); and in s.173(1) 'the specified date for compliance' means the date for compliance specified in the section in question.

Origin: 1993 s.49(1) (part), Sch.5A para.14(1) (part), (2), (3), (4); 2006 Sch.8 para.142 (part)

(3)   It is a defence, where a person is charged with an offence under s.173(1), to prove that the person took all reasonable steps for securing that the requirement in question would be complied with in time.

Origin: 1993 s.49(3); 2006 Sch.8 para.142 (part)

(4)   A person guilty of an offence under s.173(1) is liable on summary conviction to –

(a) a fine not exceeding level 4 on the standard scale, and

(b) for continued contravention, a daily default fine not exceeding 10% of level 4 on the standard scale for so long as the person in question remains a charity trustee of the charity.

Origin: 1993 s.49(1) (part), (2); 2006 Sch.8 para.142 (part)

CHAPTER 5: POWERS TO SET FINANCIAL THRESHOLDS

174   Powers to alter certain sums specified in this Part

(1)   The Minister may by order amend any provision listed in s.174(2) –

(a) by substituting a different sum for the sum for the time being specified in that provision, or

(b) if the provision specifies more than one sum, by substituting a different sum for any sum specified in that provision.

Origin: 1993 s.42(6) (part), s.43(8) (part), s.45(9) (part), s.48(4) (part); DCOA 1994 s.29(6) (part), s.30(4) (part); 2006 s.28(6) (part); SI 2006/2951 Sch.0 para.4(q), (t), (u)

(2)   The provisions are –

- s.133 (gross income in connection with option to prepare account and statement instead of statement of accounts);

- s.144(1)(a) or (b) (gross income and value of assets in connection with requirements as to audit of larger charities);

- s.145(1) (gross income in connection with option to have accounts examined instead of audited);

- s.145(3) (gross income in connection with requirements as to qualifications of independent examiner);

- s.163(1) or (2) (gross income in connection with requirements to transmit annual report to Commission);

- s.169(2) (gross income in connection with requirement to prepare annual return).

Origin: 1993 s.42(6) (part), s.43(8) (part), s.45(9) (part), s.48(4) (part); DCOA 1994 s.29(6) (part), s.30(4) (part); 2006 s.28(6) (part)

175   **Aggregate gross income of group**

The Minister may by regulations make provision for determining for the purposes of this Part the amount of the aggregate gross income for a financial year of a group consisting of a parent charity and its subsidiary undertaking or undertakings.

Origin: 1993 Sch.5A para.15; 2006 Sch.6 (part)

176   **Larger groups: 'relevant income threshold' and 'relevant assets threshold'**

(1)   The reference to the relevant income threshold in para.(a) or (b) of s.151(1) is a reference to the sum prescribed as the relevant income threshold for the purposes of that paragraph.

Origin: 1993 Sch.5A para.6(2) (part); 2006 Sch.6 (part)

(2)   The reference to the relevant assets threshold in para.(b) of s.151(1) is a reference to the sum prescribed as the relevant assets threshold for the purposes of that paragraph.

Origin: 1993 Sch.5A para.6(2) (part); 2006 Sch.6 (part)

(3)   Prescribed. means prescribed by regulations made by the Minister.

Origin: 1993 Sch.5A para.6(2) (part); 2006 Sch.6 (part)

THE CHARITIES (ACCOUNTS AND REPORTS) REGULATIONS 2008 (S.I.2008/629)

Reg. 8: Form and content of statement of accounts ... –

(1)   This regulation applies to a statement of accounts prepared by the charity trustees of a charity which is not an investment fund or a special case charity in accordance with [section 132(1) of the 2011 Act].

(2)   The requirements as to form and content of a statement of accounts to which this regulation applies are prescribed in paragraphs (3) to (11).

(3)   The statement of accounts must consist of –

    (a)   a statement of financial activities showing the total incoming resources and application of the resources, together with any other movements in the total resources, of the charity during the relevant financial year; and

    (b)   a balance sheet showing the state of affairs of the charity as at the end of the relevant financial year.

(4)   The statement of accounts must be prepared in accordance with the following principles –

    (a)   the statement of financial activities must give a true and fair view of the incoming resources and application of the resources of the charity in the relevant financial year;

    (b)   the balance sheet must give a true and fair view of the state of affairs of the charity at the end of the relevant financial year;

    (c)   where compliance with paragraphs (5) to (10) would not be sufficient to give a true and fair view as required under sub-paragraph (a) or (b), the additional information necessary to give a true and fair view must be given in the statement of accounts or in notes to the accounts;

    (d)   if in special circumstances compliance with any of the requirements of paragraphs (5) to (10) would be inconsistent with giving a true and fair view, the charity trustees must depart from the relevant requirement to the extent necessary to give a true and fair view.

(5)   The statement of accounts must be prepared in accordance with the methods and principles set out in the SORP.

(6)   Subject to paragraphs (7) to (9), the statement of accounts must, in relation to any amount required to be shown in the statement of financial activities or in the balance sheet for the relevant financial year, show the corresponding amount for the financial year immediately preceding the relevant financial year.

(7)   Where a charity has more than one fund, only amounts corresponding to the entries in the statement of financial activities relating to the totals of both or all of the funds of the charity need be shown.

(8)   Where the corresponding amount referred to in paragraph (6) is not comparable with the amount to be shown for the item in question in respect of the relevant financial year, the corresponding amount is to be adjusted.

(9)   Where –

    (a)   the effect of paragraphs (4) and (5) is that there is nothing to be shown in respect of a particular item for the relevant financial year; but

    (b)   an amount was required to be shown in respect of that item in the statement of accounts for the financial year immediately preceding the relevant financial year, paragraphs (4) and (5) have effect as if an amount were required to be shown in the statement of accounts for the relevant financial year, and that amount were nil.

(10) There must be provided by way of notes to the accounts the information specified in Schedule 2*.

(11) The balance sheet must –

   (a) be signed by at least one of the charity trustees of the charity, each of whom has been authorised to do so; and

   (b) specify the date on which the statement of accounts of which the balance sheet forms part was approved by the charity trustees.

*Schedule 2: Notes to the Statement of Accounts …

(1) Subject to sub-paragraphs (2) and (3) and in so far as it is not provided in the statement of financial activities or in the balance sheet, the information to be provided by way of notes to the accounts is—

   (a) particulars of any material adjustment made under regulation 8(8);

   (b) a description of –

      (i) each of the accounting policies which (aa) have been adopted by the charity trustees; and

      (bb) are material in the context of the accounts of the charity; and

      (ii) the estimation techniques adopted by the charity trustees which are material to the presentation of the accounts;

   (c) a description of any material change to policies and techniques referred to in paragraph (b), the reason for such change and its effect (if material) on the accounts, in accordance with the methods and principles set out in the SORP;

   (d) a description of the nature and purpose of all material funds of the charity in accordance with the methods and principles set out in the SORP;

   (e) such particulars of transactions of the charity, or of any subsidiary undertaking of the charity, entered into with a related party as are required to be disclosed by the SORP;

   (f) such particulars of the cost to the charity of employing and providing pensions for staff as are required by the SORP to be disclosed;

   (g) such particulars of the emoluments of staff employed by the charity as may be required by the SORP to be disclosed;

   (h) a description of any incoming resources which represent capital, according to whether or not that capital is permanent endowment;

   (i) an itemised analysis of any material movement between any of the restricted funds of the charity, or between a restricted and an unrestricted fund of the charity, together with an explanation of the nature and purpose of each of those funds;

   (j) the name of any subsidiary undertaking of the charity, together with a description of the nature of the charity's relationship with that subsidiary undertaking, and of its activities, and, where material, a statement of the turnover and net profit or loss of the subsidiary undertaking for the corresponding financial year and any qualification expressed in an auditor's report on the accounts of the subsidiary undertaking for that financial year;

   (k) particulars of any guarantee given by the charity, where any potential liability under the guarantee is outstanding at the date of the balance sheet;

   (l) particulars of any loan outstanding at the date of the balance sheet –

      (i) which was made to the charity and which is secured by an express charge on any of the assets of the charity; or

(ii) which was made by the charity to any subsidiary undertaking of the charity;

(m) particulars of any fund of the charity which is in deficit at the date of the balance sheet;

(n) particulars of any remuneration paid to an auditor or independent examiner in respect of auditing or examining the accounts of the charity and particulars of any remuneration paid to the auditor or independent examiner in respect of any other services rendered to the charity;

(o) subject to paragraph (2), such particulars of any grant made by the charity as may be required by the SORP to be disclosed;

(p) particulars of any ex gratia payment made by the charity;

(q) an analysis of any entry in the statement of financial activities relating to resources expended on charitable activities as may be required by the SORP to be disclosed;

(r) such particulars of any support costs incurred by the charity as may be required by the SORP to be disclosed;

(s) an analysis of any entry in the balance sheet relating to –

(i) fixed assets;

(ii) debtors;

(iii) creditors,

according to the categories set out in the SORP;

(t) an analysis of all material changes during the financial year in question in the values of fixed assets, in accordance with the methods and principles set out in the SORP;

(u) in the case of any amount required by any of the preceding sub-paragraphs other than sub-paragraph (i), (o) or (t) to be disclosed, the corresponding amount for the financial year immediately preceding the relevant financial year;

(v) a statement as to whether or not the accounts have been prepared in accordance with any applicable accounting standards and statements of recommended practice and particulars of any material departure from those standards and statements of practice and the reasons for such departure;

(w) where the charity trustees have exercised their powers under regulation 3(4)(b) so as to determine an accounting reference date earlier or later than 12 months from the beginning of the financial year, a statement of their reasons for doing so;

(x) if, in accordance with regulation 8(4)(d), the charity trustees have departed from any requirement of regulation 8, particulars of any such departure, the reasons for it, and its effect; and

(y) any additional information which –

(i) is required to ensure that the statement of accounts complies with the requirements of regulation 8; or

(ii) may reasonably assist the user to understand the statement of accounts.

(2) The charity trustees of a charity that is a charitable trust created by any person ('the settler') are not required to disclose under paragraph (o) of sub-paragraph (1) any excepted information if the disclosure of that information would fall to be made at a time when (a) the settlor; or (b) the spouse or civil partner of the settlor, is still alive.

(3) In this Schedule –

(a) 'corresponding financial year' has the meaning given by regulation 9(3);

(b) 'excepted information' means –

(i) the identities of recipients of grants made out of the funds of the charity;

(ii) the amounts of individual grants so made.

Preparation of group accounts

Reg. 9: Meaning of 'aggregate gross income'

(1)   ... the aggregate gross income for a financial year of a group consisting of a parent charity and its subsidiary undertaking or undertakings is to be determined by eliminating all group transactions for that year from the group income for that year.

(2)   For the purposes of this regulation –

    (a) 'corresponding financial year' has the meaning given by paragraph (3);

    (b) 'gross income' means, in relation to a non-charitable subsidiary undertaking, the amount of income of that undertaking that would be construed as its gross income were it a charity;

    (c) 'group income' means the aggregate of –

        (i)   the gross income of the parent charity for the financial year;

        (ii) the gross income of each charitable subsidiary undertaking of that parent charity for the corresponding financial year; and

        (iii) the gross income of each non-charitable subsidiary undertaking of that parent charity for the corresponding financial year.

    (d) 'group transactions' means –

        (i)   all income and expenditure relating to transactions between members of the group;

        (ii) all gains and losses relating to transactions between members of the group;

    (e) 'member of a group' is to be construed in accordance with [section 141 of the 2011 Act];

(3)   Subject to paragraph (4), 'corresponding financial year' in relation to a subsidiary undertaking means –

    (a) in the case of a subsidiary undertaking whose financial year ends with that of the parent charity, that year;

    (b) in any other case, the financial year of the subsidiary undertaking ending immediately before the end of the financial year of the parent charity.

(4)   If the figures for the corresponding financial year of a subsidiary undertaking cannot be obtained without disproportionate expense or undue delay, the latest available figures are to be taken.

10   Financial years of subsidiary undertakings

(1)   For the purposes of [section 141(3) of the 2011 Act] the financial years of subsidiary undertakings are to be determined in accordance with this regulation.

(2)   The financial year of a charitable subsidiary undertaking is to be determined in accordance with section [353(1) of the 2011] Act.

(3)   The financial year of a non-charitable subsidiary undertaking is a period in respect of which a profit and loss account of the undertaking is required to be made up (by its constitution or by the law under which it is established), whether that period is a year or not.

11   Requirement for financial years of a parent charity and its subsidiary undertakings to coincide

The charity trustees of a parent charity must secure that, except where in their opinion there are good reasons against it, the financial year of each of its subsidiary undertakings coincides with its own financial year.

15 Form and content of group accounts...

(1)   ...

(2)   The form and content of the group accounts to which this regulation applies are prescribed in paragraphs (3) to (5) and regulation 16.

(3)   The group accounts must consist of –

(a)   a consolidated statement of financial activities showing the total incoming resources and application of the resources, together with any other movements in the total resources, of the parent charity and its subsidiary undertakings in the relevant financial year; and

(b)   a consolidated balance sheet showing the state of affairs of the parent charity and its subsidiary undertakings as at the end of the relevant financial year.

(4)   The group accounts must be prepared in accordance with the following principles –

a)   the consolidated statement of financial activities must give a true and fair view of the total incoming resources of the parent charity and its subsidiary undertakings and the movements in the total resources of the group during the relevant financial year;

(b)   the consolidated balance sheet gives a true and fair view of the state of affairs of the parent charity and its undertakings as at the end of the relevant financial year.

(5)   The group accounts prepared under this regulation must –

(a)   so far as practicable comply with the requirements of paragraphs (6) to (10) of regulation 8 as if parent charity and its subsidiary undertakings were a single charity; ...

16 Form and content of group accounts: general requirements

(1)   In addition to complying with regulation 13 ... the group accounts prepared by the charity trustees of any parent charity under [section 138(2) of the 2011 Act] must comply with the requirements prescribed in this regulation.

(2)   The group accounts must be prepared in accordance with applicable accounting principles and in particular must make the adjustments or include the information prescribed in this regulation.

(3)   The group accounts must incorporate in full the information contained in the individual accounts of the parent charity and its relevant subsidiary undertakings, subject to such consolidation adjustments, if any, as may be appropriate in accordance with applicable accounting principles.

(4)   Where the financial year of a relevant subsidiary undertaking differs from that of the parent charity, the group accounts must be made up from –

(a)   the accounts of the relevant subsidiary undertaking for its most recent financial year ending before the last day of the parent financial year, provided that financial year ended no more than three months before the parent financial year ended; or

(b)   interim accounts prepared by the relevant subsidiary undertaking as at the end of the parent financial year.

(5)   Where an undertaking becomes a subsidiary undertaking of a parent charity, that event must be accounted for in the group accounts by the acquisition method or merger method of accounting as appropriate in accordance with applicable accounting principles.

(6)   Where the parent charity or a relevant subsidiary undertaking –

(a)   has an interest in an associated undertaking or participates in the management of a joint venture and that associated undertaking or joint venture is not itself a subsidiary undertaking of the parent charity; or

(b) participates in a joint arrangement, the interest of the parent charity or subsidiary undertaking in that associated undertaking, joint venture or joint arrangement must appear in the group accounts as appropriate in accordance with applicable accounting principles.

(7) The consolidated balance sheet must identify as a separate item any minority interest in the net assets or liabilities of any relevant subsidiary undertaking as appropriate in accordance with applicable accounting principles.

(8) The consolidated statement of financial activities, consolidated income and expenditure account or consolidated statement of changes in net assets, as relevant, must identify as a separate item any minority interest in the net movement of the funds of a relevant subsidiary undertaking as appropriate in accordance with applicable accounting principles.

(9) In this regulation –

(a) 'applicable accounting principles' means, in relation to a parent charity that is required to prepare group accounts, the methods and principles set out in –

(i) the financial reporting standards and statements of standard accounting practice issued by the body known as The Accounting Standards Board(a) ('the Board') that are relevant to the preparation of those accounts by that parent charity;

(ii) any abstract issued by the committee of the Board known as the Urgent Issues Task Force which is relevant to the preparation of those accounts by that parent charity; and

(iii) any statement of recommended practice (including the SORP) issued by a body recognised by the Board for the purpose of issuing guidance on the standards in paragraph (i) relevant to the preparation of those accounts by that parent charity.

(b) 'parent financial year' means the financial year of the parent charity in respect of which the group accounts are prepared;

(c) 'relevant subsidiary undertaking' means a subsidiary undertaking of the parent charity which is not excluded under regulation 19 from the group accounts required to be prepared for the parent financial year.

17   Group accounts: departure from the general rules

(1) Where compliance with the group accounts requirements is not sufficient to comply with any requirement to give a true and fair view, the necessary additional information must be given in the group accounts or a note to them.

(2) If in special circumstances compliance with any of the group accounts requirements is inconsistent with a requirement to give a true and fair view, the charity trustees must depart from the relevant provision to the extent necessary to give a true and fair view.

(3) Particulars of any departure under paragraph (2), the reasons for it and its effect must be given in a note to the group accounts.

(4) In this regulation 'group accounts requirements' mean the requirements prescribed by regulation 13 … and regulation 16.

Exceptions relating to requirement to prepare group accounts

18   The sum specified for the purposes of [section 139(2) of the 2011 Act] is £500,000.

19(1) The circumstances in which a subsidiary undertaking may be excluded from group accounts required to be prepared under [section 138(2) of the 2011 Act] are –

(a) subject to paragraph (2), where the inclusion of the subsidiary undertaking is not material for the purposes of giving a true and fair view;

(b)   severe long term restrictions substantially hinder the exercise of the rights of the parent charity over the assets or management of the undertaking;

(c)   the information which is necessary for the preparation of the group accounts cannot be obtained without disproportionate expense or undue delay;

(d)   the interest of the parent charity in the undertaking is held exclusively with a view to subsequent resale.

(2)   Two or more subsidiary undertakings may only be excluded from the group accounts under paragraph (1)(a) if they are not material when taken together.

34   Dispensations from audit or examination requirements

(1)   The Commission may –

(a)   in the circumstances specified in paragraph (2), dispense with the requirements of [sections 144(2) or 145(1) of the 2011 Act] in the case of a particular charity;

(b)   in the circumstances specified in paragraph (3) dispense with those requirements in respect of a particular financial year of a charity;

(c)   in the circumstances specified in paragraph (4) dispense with the requirements in [section 151(4)(a) of the 2011 Act] in the case of a particular charity;

(d)   in the circumstances specified in paragraph (5) dispense with those requirements in respect of a particular financial year of a charity.

(2)   The circumstances specified for the purposes of paragraph (1)(a) are where the Commission is satisfied that the accounts of the charity concerned –

(a)   are required to be audited in accordance with any statutory provision contained in or having effect under an Act of Parliament which imposes requirements which, in the opinion of the Commission, are sufficiently similar to the requirements of [section 144(2)] for those requirements to be dispensed with;

(b)   have been audited by the Comptroller and Auditor General or the Auditor General for Wales.

(3)   The circumstances specified for the purposes of paragraph (1)(b) are where the Commission –

(a)   is satisfied that the accounts of the charity concerned for the financial year in question have been, or will be, audited or examined in accordance with requirements or arrangements which, in the opinion of the Commission, are sufficiently similar to the relevant requirements of [section 145 of the 2011 Act] applicable to that financial year of that charity for those requirements to be dispensed with;

(b)   considers that, although the financial year in question of the charity concerned is one to which [section 144(2) of the 2011 Act] applies, there are exceptional circumstances which justify the examination of the accounts by an independent examiner instead of their audit in accordance with that subsection.

(4)   The circumstances specified for the purposes of paragraph (1)(c) are where the Commission is satisfied that the group accounts of the parent charity concerned –

(a)   are required to be audited in accordance with any statutory provision contained in or having effect under an Act of Parliament which imposes requirements which, in the opinion of the Commission, are sufficiently similar to the requirements of [section 151(4)(a)] for those requirements to be dispensed with;

(b)   have been audited by the Comptroller and Auditor General or the Auditor General for Wales.

(5)   The circumstances specified for the purpose of paragraph (1)(d) are where the Commission is satisfied that the group accounts of the parent charity concerned for the financial year in question have been, or will be, audited in accordance with requirements or arrangements which, in the opinion of the

Commission, are sufficiently similar to the requirements of [section 151(4)(a)] for those requirements to be dispensed with.

(6)   The Commission must make it a condition of a dispensation granted under this regulation that the charity trustees send to the Commission any report made to the trustees with respect to the accounts of that charity for the relevant financial year of which it requests a copy.

(7)   The Commission must make it a condition of a dispensation granted under paragraph (3)(b) that the charity trustees comply with the requirements of [section 145 of the 2011 Act] as if they were able to make and had in fact made an election under that section that the accounts of the charity for the relevant financial year be examined by an independent examiner.

(8)   The Commission may revoke a dispensation granted under this regulation if the charity trustees fail to comply with a condition imposed under paragraph (6) or (7).

40   Annual reports: non-parent charity

(1)   This regulation applies to an annual report prepared in accordance with [section 162(1) of the 2011 Act] by the charity trustees of a non-parent charity.

(2)   The report on the activities of a charity during the year which is required to be contained in the annual report prepared under [section 162] –

(a)   must specify the financial year to which it relates;

(b)   must –

(i)   in the case of a charity which is not an auditable charity, be a brief summary setting out (aa) the main activities undertaken by the charity to further its charitable purposes for the public benefit; and (bb) the main achievements of the charity during the year.

(ii) in the case of a charity which is an auditable charity, be a review of the significant activities undertaken by the charity during the relevant financial year to further its charitable purposes for the public benefit or to generate resources to be used to further its purposes including –

(aa)   details of the aims and objectives which the charity trustees have set for the charity in that year, details of the strategies adopted and of significant activities undertaken, in order to achieve those aims and objectives;

(bb)   details of the achievements of the charity during the year, measured by reference to the aims and objectives which have been set;

(cc)   details of any significant contribution of volunteers to these activities;

(dd)   details of the principal sources of income of the charity; and

(ee)   a statement as to whether the charity trustees have given consideration to the major risks to which the charity is exposed and satisfied themselves that systems or procedures are established in order to manage those risks;

(c)   must –

(i)   where (aa) any fund of the charity was in deficit at the beginning of the relevant financial; and (bb) the charity is one in respect of which a statement of accounts has been prepared under [section 133(1) of the 2011 Act] for that financial year, contain particulars of the steps taken by the charity trustees to eliminate that deficit;

(ii) contain a statement by the charity trustees as to whether they have complied with the duty in [section 17(5) of the 2011 Act] to have due regard to guidance published by the Commission; and

(iii) be dated and be signed by one or more of the charity trustees, each of whom has been authorised to do so.

(3)   Subject to paragraphs (4) to (7), the other information relating to a charity and to its trustees and officers which is required to be contained in the annual report is –

(a)   the name of the charity as it appears in the register of charities and any other name by which it makes itself known;

(b)   the number assigned to it in the register ...;

(c)   the principal address of the charity ...;

(d)   the name of any person who is a charity trustee of the charity on the date when the authority referred to in paragraph (2)(c)(iii) above is given, and, where any charity trustee on that date is a body corporate, the name of any person who is a director of the body corporate on that date;

(e)   the name of any other person who has, at any time during the relevant financial year been a charity trustee of the charity;

(f)   the name of any person who is a trustee for the charity on the date referred to in sub-paragraph (d);

(g)   the name of any other person who has, at any time during the relevant financial year been a trustee for the charity;

(h)   particulars, including the date if known, of any deed or other document containing provisions which regulate the purposes and administration of the charity;

(i)   the name of any person or body of persons entitled by the trusts of the charity to appoint one or more new charity trustees and a description of the method provided by those trusts for such appointment;

(j)   a description of the policies and procedures (if any) which have been adopted by the charity trustees for the induction and training of charity trustees and where no such policies have been adopted a statement to that effect;

(k)   a description of the organisational structure of the charity;

(l)   a summary description of the purposes of the charity;

(m)   a description of the policies (if any) which have been adopted by the charity trustees for the selection of individuals and institutions who are to receive grants or other forms of financial support out of the assets of the charity;

(n)   a statement regarding the performance during the financial year of the investments belonging to the charity (if any);

(o)   where material investments are owned by a charity, a description of the policies (if any) which have been adopted by the charity trustees for the selection, retention and realization of investments for the charity including the extent (if any) to which social, environmental or ethical considerations are taken into account;

(p)   a description of the policies (if any) which have been adopted by the charity trustees for the purpose of determining the level of reserves which it is appropriate for the charity to maintain in order to meet effectively the needs designated by its trusts, together with details of the amount and purpose of any material commitments and planned expenditure not provided for in the balance sheet which have been deducted from the assets in the unrestricted fund of the charity in calculating the amount of reserves, and where no such policies have been adopted, a statement to that effect;

(q)   a description of the aims and objectives which the charity trustees have set for the charity in the future and of the activities contemplated in furtherance of those aims and objectives;

(r)   a description of any assets held by the charity or by any charity trustee of, or trustee for, the charity, on behalf of another charity, and particulars of any special arrangements made with respect to the safe custody of such assets and their segregation from assets of the charity not so held and a description of the objects of the charity on whose behalf the assets are held.

(4)   The Commission may, where it is satisfied that, in the case of a particular charity or class of charities, or in the case of a particular financial year of a charity or class of charities –

    (a) the disclosure of the name of any person whose name is required by any of sub-paragraphs (d), (e), (f), (g) and (i) of paragraph (3) to be contained in the annual report of a charity could lead to that person being placed in any personal danger, dispense with the requirement in any of those sub-paragraphs so far as it applies to the name of such person;

    (b) the disclosure of the principal address of the charity in accordance with paragraph (3)(c) above could lead to any such person being placed in any personal danger, dispense with that requirement.

(5)   In the case of a charity having more than 50 charity trustees on the date referred to in paragraph (3)(d) –

    (a) paragraph (3)(d) has effect as if for 'name of any person who is a charity trustee of the charity' there were substituted 'names of not less than 50 of the charity trustees of the charity, including any charity trustee who is also an officer of the charity'; and

    (b) paragraph (3)(e) has effect as if, at the end of that paragraph, there were inserted 'other than the name of any charity trustee whose name has been excluded from the report in pursuance of sub-paragraph (d)'.

(6)   In the case of a report prepared under [section 168(3) of the 2011 Act] (excepted charities which are not registered), paragraph (4) has effect as if –

    (a) in sub-paragraph (a) from 'as it appears in the register of charities' to the end; and

    (b) in sub-paragraph (b) 'the number assigned to it in the register and,', were omitted.

(7)   Sub-paragraphs (j), (k), (m), (n), (o) and (q) of paragraph (3) do not apply to a charity which is not an auditable charity.

41   Annual Reports: qualifying parent charities

(1)   This regulation applies to an annual report prepared in accordance with [section 162(1) of the 2011 Act] by the charity trustees of a qualifying parent charity.

(2)   The report on the activities of such a parent charity and its subsidiary undertakings, during the year, which is required to be contained in the annual report prepared under [section 162] in respect of each financial year of the charity must –

    (a) specify the financial year to which it relates;

    (b) be a review of the significant activities undertaken by the charity during the relevant financial year to further its charitable purposes for the public benefit or to generate resources to be used to further its purposes including details of –

        (i)   the aims and objectives which the charity trustees have set for the parent charity and its subsidiary undertakings in that year;

        (ii) the strategies adopted and the significant activities undertaken, in order to achieve those aims and objectives;

        (iii) the achievements of the parent charity and its subsidiary undertakings during the year, measured by reference to the aims and objectives which have been set,

        (iv) any significant contribution of volunteers to these activities; and

        (v)   the principal sources of income of the parent charity and of its subsidiary undertakings;

    (c) contain a statement as to whether the charity trustees have –

        (i)   given consideration to the major risks to which the parent charity and its subsidiary undertakings are exposed; and

(ii) satisfied themselves that systems or procedures are established in order to manage those risks;

(d) where any fund of the parent charity was in deficit at the beginning of the financial year in question, contain particulars of the steps taken by the charity trustees to eliminate that deficit;

(e) where the total of capital and reserves in any of the parent charity's subsidiary undertakings was materially in deficit at the beginning of the financial year, contain particulars of the steps taken by the relevant undertaking or undertakings to eliminate that deficit,

(f) contain a statement by the charity trustees as to whether they have complied with the duty in [section 17(5) of the 2011 Act] to have due regard to guidance published by the Commission; and

(g) be dated and be signed by one or more of the charity trustees, each of whom has been authorised to do so.

(3) Subject to paragraphs (4) to (6), the information relating to a qualifying parent charity, to its trustees and officers, and to its subsidiary undertakings, which is required to be contained in the annual report is –

(a) the name of the parent charity as it appears in the register of charities and any other name by which it makes itself known;

(b) the number assigned to the parent charity in the register ...;

(c) the principal address of the parent charity ...;

(d) the name of any person who is a charity trustee of the parent charity on the date when the authority referred to in paragraph (2)(g) is given, and, where any charity trustee on that date is a body corporate, the name of any person who is a director of the body corporate on that date;

(e) the name of any other person who has, at any time during the financial year in question, been a charity trustee of the parent charity;

(f) the name of any person who is a trustee for the parent charity on the date referred to in sub-paragraph (d);

(g) the name of any other person who has, at any time during the financial year in question, been a trustee for the parent charity;

(h) particulars, including the date if known, of any deed or other document containing provisions which regulate the purposes and administration of the parent charity;

(i) the name of any person or body of persons entitled by the trusts of the parent charity to appoint one or more new charity trustees, and a description of the method provided by those trusts for such appointment;

(j) a description of the policies and procedures (if any) which have been adopted by the charity trustees of the parent charity for the induction and training of charity trustees, and where no such policies have been adopted a statement to this effect;

(k) a description of the organisational structure of the parent charity and of its subsidiary undertakings;

(l) a summary description of the purposes of the parent charity;

(m) a description of the policies (if any) which have been adopted by the charity trustees of the parent charity for the selection of individuals and institutions who are to receive grants, or other forms of financial support, out of the assets of the charity;

(n) a statement regarding the performance during the financial year of –

(i) any investments belonging to the parent charity; and

(ii) any investments belonging to the parent charity's subsidiary undertakings, where those investments are material to the group accounts;

    (o) where –

        (i) investments are owned by a qualifying parent charity or any of its subsidiary undertakings; and

        (ii) those investments are material to the group accounts, a description of the policies (if any) which have been adopted by the charity trustees, or as the case may be the subsidiary undertaking, for the selection, retention and realization of investments, including the extent (if any) to which social, environmental or ethical considerations are taken into account;

    (p) where the charity trustees have adopted polices for the purpose of determining the level of reserves which it is appropriate to maintain in order to meet effectively the needs designated by its trusts –

        (i) a description of those policies including in particular whether account has been taken of any reserves held by its subsidiary undertakings in determining the appropriate level of reserves;

        (ii) details of the amount and purpose of any material commitments and planned expenditure not provided for in the balance sheet which have been deducted from the assets in the unrestricted fund of the charity in calculating the amount of reserves;

    (q) if the charity trustees have not adopted policies falling within sub-paragraph (p), a statement that no such policies have been adopted;

    (r) a description of the aims and objectives which the charity trustees have set for the parent charity in the future, and of the activities contemplated in furtherance of those aims and objectives;

    (s) a description of any assets held by the parent charity or by any charity trustee of, or trustee for, the charity, on behalf of another charity, and particulars of any special arrangements made with respect to the safe custody of such assets and their segregation from assets of the charity not so held and a description of the objects of the charity on whose behalf the assets are held.

(4)   The Commission may, where it is satisfied that, in the case of a particular charity or class of charities, or in the case of a particular financial year of a charity or class of charities –

    (a) the disclosure of the name of any person whose name is required by any of subparagraphs (d), (e), (f), (g) and (i) of paragraph (3) above to be contained in the annual report of a charity could lead to that person being placed in any personal danger, dispense with the requirement in any of those sub-paragraphs so far as it applies to the name of that person; or

    (b) the disclosure of the principal address of the charity in accordance with paragraph (3)(c)above could lead to any such person being placed in any personal danger, dispense with that requirement.

(5)   In the case of a charity having more than 50 charity trustees on the date referred to in paragraph (3)(d) –

    (a) that sub-paragraph has effect as if for the words 'name of any person who is a charity trustee of the charity' there were substituted the words 'names of not less than 50 of the charity trustees of the charity, including any charity trustee who is also an officer of the charity'; and

    (b) paragraph (3)(e) has effect as if, at the end of the sub-paragraph, there were inserted the words 'other than the name of any charity trustee whose name has been excluded from the report in pursuance of sub-paragraph (d)'.

(6)   In the case of a report prepared under [section 168(3) of the 2011 Act] (excepted charities which are not registered), paragraph (3) above shall have effect as if –

    (a) in sub-paragraph (a) the words from 'as it appears in the register of charities' to the end, and

    (b) in sub-paragraph (b) the words 'the number assigned to it in the register and,', were omitted.

(7)   In this regulation, 'subsidiary undertaking' does not include a subsidiary undertaking which is excluded from the group accounts in accordance with regulation 19.

Church Representation Rules

Parochial Church Meetings and Councils

Business

9.(1)   The annual meeting shall receive from the parochial church council and shall be free to discuss

(a)   a report on changes in the roll since the last annual parochial church meeting or, in a year in which a new roll is prepared, a report on the numbers entered on the new roll;

(b)   an annual report on the proceedings of the parochial church council and the activities of the parish generally;

(c)   the financial statements of the parochial church council for the year ending on the 31 December immediately preceding the meeting, independently examined or audited as provided by paragraph (3) hereof;

(d)   a report upon the fabric, goods and ornaments of the church or churches of the parish under section 5 of the Care of Churches and Ecclesiastical Jurisdiction Measure 1991; and

(e)   a report on the proceedings of the deanery synod.

(2)   The council shall cause a copy of the said roll to be available for inspection at the meeting.

(3)   The said financial statements shall –

(a)   be independently examined or audited in such manner as shall be prescribed in accordance with rule 54(8);

(b)   be considered and, if thought fit, approved by the parochial church council and signed by the chairman presiding at the meeting of the council; and

(c)   be displayed for a continuous period of at least seven days before the annual meeting, including at least one Sunday when the church is used for worship, on a notice-board either inside or outside the church.

(4)   The annual report referred to in paragraph (1)(b) above and the said financial statements shall be prepared in such form as shall be prescribed in accordance with rule 54(8) hereof for consideration by the annual meeting. Following such meeting the council shall cause copies of the annual report and statements to be sent within twenty-eight days of the annual meeting to the secretary of the diocesan board of finance for retention by the board.

(5)   The annual meeting shall in the manner provided by rule 11 –

(a)   lect in every third year parochial representatives of the laity to the deanery synod;

(b)   elect parochial representatives of the laity to the parochial church council;

(c)   appoint sidesmen;

(d)   appoint the independent examiner or auditor to the council for a term of office ending at the close of the next annual meeting, provided that such person shall not be a member of the council; and the elections and appointments shall be carried out in the above order.

Supplementary and interpretation

54.(8)

(a)   In these rules any matters or regulations to be prescribed shall be prescribed by the Business Committee of the General Synod in accordance with the following procedure.

(b)   Any matters or regulations made under this rule shall be laid before the General Synod and shall not come into force until they have been approved by the General Synod, whether with or without amendment.

(c)   Where the Business Committee determines that matters or regulations made under this rule do not need to be debated by the General Synod then, unless –

(i)   notice is given by a member of the General Synod in accordance with Standing Orders that he wishes the business to be debated, or

(ii)   notice is so given by any such member that he wishes to move an amendment to the business, the matters or regulations shall for the proposes of sub-paragraph (b) above be deemed to have been approved by the General Synod without amendment.

General provisions relating to parochial church councils

Officers of the Council

1. (g)   If an independent examiner or auditor to the council is not appointed by the annual meeting or if an independent examiner or auditor appointed by the annual meeting is unable or unwilling to act, an independent examiner or auditor (who shall not be a member of the council) shall be appointed by the council for a term of office ending at the close of the next annual meeting. The remuneration (if any) of the independent examiner or auditor shall be paid by the council.

Minutes

12. (e)   The independent examiner or auditor of the council's financial statements, the bishop, the archdeacon and any person authorised by one of them in writing shall have access to the approved minutes of the council meetings without the authority of the council.

Acknowledgements

The support of the following members of the Diocesan Accounts Sub-groups in preparing this guide is gratefully acknowledged:

Ashley Ellis, (Chairperson), Diocesan Secretary, Wakefield Diocese

Heather Burge, PA to the Diocesan Secretary, Wakefield Diocese

Greyham Dawes, Director – Not-for-profit Unit, Crowe Clark Whitehill LLP

Paul Gibson, National Charity Specialist, Charity Sector & Social Enterprise Group, Mazars LLP

Shelagh Ibbs, Director, Data Developments (UK) Limited

Bryan Lewis, Deputy Diocesan Secretary & Finance Manager, Wakefield Diocese

Mary Makin, Diocesan Accountant, Guildford, Portsmouth and Winchester Dioceses

Ronald Norey, Secretary, Association of Church Accountants & Treasurers

Roger Pinchbeck, Deputy Diocesan Secretary & Finance Officer, Sheffield Diocese

John Preston, National Stewardship and Resources Officer, Church of England

Katy Reade, Diocesan Accountant, St Edmundsbury & Ipswich Diocese

Index

Index to Part 2

Index created by Meg Davies (Fellow of the Society of Indexers)